CONTENTS

ABOUT THE AUTHOR

Tobe Aleksander is a writer and broadcaster on a wide range of consumer, legal and financial issues. She has worked with the Citizens Advice Bureau as a professional adviser. She also teaches assertiveness and communication skills. Her books include: *The Assertive Consumer – An everyday guide to your rights at home, work and in the high street* (1990); *The Complete Guide to Living Together* (1992); *The Right to be Yourself* (1992); *His, Hers, Theirs – A financial guide for stepfamilies* (1995).

Acknowledgements

The author's thanks go to Nicholas Aleksander, Elspeth Chapman, Vinnette Marshall and Lesley Williams and to the many women who contributed their experiences to this book including Margaret Adams, Mary Cleary, Christine Lloyd, Joy Peach, Sheila Russell Davies, Pamela Spencer and Gwyn Williamson.

Age Concern acknowledges the kind support of Barclays Bank in the production of this book.

Introduction

Over one in three marriages now ends in divorce. Throughout the 1970s and 1980s the number of people aged over 45 who separated or divorced almost doubled. The vast majority of divorces are initiated by women. Yet, for all the statistics, many people still regard the public failure of their marriage as an embarrassment and a social stigma.

Twenty-five, thirty, even forty years of married life may represent more than half your current life-span. Loosening the ties and trappings of marriage can be an exceedingly painful experience. For older women who have become dependent on – if perhaps not altogether trustful of – their married state, separation and divorce can be daunting, possibly devastating.

Managing the dissolution of your marriage and setting out on your own is a huge challenge. For those who feel they have no marketable skills or are ending their working life or are already retired, the financial implications of parting are considerable. So too are the emotional ones – the sense of rejection perhaps, or the feeling of failure or utter hopelessness. Yet, as many of the women whose voices are heard in this book will testify, divorce and separation can also be tremendously liberating.

The aim of this book is to provide a practical guide through the legal and financial maze of separation and divorce. It is not intended as a definitive 'do it yourself' handbook, although there is plenty of advice to help you manage all or part of the process yourself. Most importantly, the book is here to enable you to know what questions to ask and where to seek information.

This book is also here to help you explore the emotional aspects of divorce and separation,

Throughout the book you will read the experiences of women who have gone through separation and divorce in later life. All real names have been changed. Many had celebrated their silver wedding anniversaries, some their ruby, before their marriages ended. Their recollections are funny as well as heart-rending. They talk openly about the good times and the bad; money, lawyers and sex as well as their hopes and fears for the future. You may find parallels in your own life. It is hoped that they will provide inspiration as well as diversion.

At the end of the book you will find a resource section. This contains the addresses of organisations mentioned in the preceding chapters as well as other sources of support and advice.

If you have just picked up this book, you are most likely to be setting out on your journey through separation and divorce, or trying to decide if your marriage has really reached this stage. The factual information may appear overwhelming, some of the comments irritatingly optimistic. At this point in your life, things might seem to be about as bad as they could ever get and you've a sneaking suspicion they could just take a turn for the worse. Yet the vast majority of women, regardless of their age, make it through to 'the other side', and on the way many positive things emerge. Take heart: one day you will probably look back and be amazed at how far you've travelled and that after all you've survived, and survived well.

NOTE The information in this book is based on the law in England and Wales. If you live in Scotland or Northern Ireland you will find certain differences in the law and common practices, and you should always check with a local lawyer or advice agency.

Future changes in the law

Wherever you live, you should be aware that there are proposals to amend many of the current laws and practices which affect the family, in particular the divorce procedure. Most of these changes are flagged in the book but it may be some years before they reach the statute books. However, you should always ask your legal adviser to explain the latest position to you.

A note for women cohabiting with their partners

This book has been written for women who are married to, rather than simply living with, their partners. If you are separating from a partner with whom you are cohabiting then your legal position will be very different. You should bear in mind the following broad principles and seek proper legal advice.

- There is no such thing as 'common law marriage'. Living together as 'man and wife' gives you no legal rights regardless of how long you have been together.

- If you separate you have no automatic right to the family home unless you are the legal owner or you have taken steps to acquire ownership.

- If you separate you have no automatic right to maintenance from your former partner.

- If you have children by your partner then you can make a claim for child maintenance in exactly the same way as if you were married.

- If your partner dies then you are highly unlikely to be able to make a claim on his estate unless you are a named beneficiary in his Will.

NOTE There are proposals to change the law to make it easier for cohabitees to inherit from their partner if the latter dies without making a Will.

1.
Facing facts

For many women facing the possibility of separation or divorce one of the questions uppermost in their minds is, 'How did it happen?' No matter how serious the ups and downs in your relationship over the years, it is never easy to come to terms with the fact that it may finally be over. A long, uncomfortable marriage may become comfortable simply through familiarity.

Most separations are like the bubbling over of a boiling pan. Marriages can simmer away for months – years even – unsatisfactory, unfulfilling, unromantic. Husbands and wives close their eyes to the other's infidelity or shut their minds to meanness or abuse, alcoholism or humiliation. They stop communicating and stop loving. Marriages like rivers can simply run dry. Then it dawns on one or both of them that they can no longer go on living together. Often it's impossible to pinpoint quite when these things occur. Silently and unmarked we – or our partners – cross the line that divides willingness to tolerate an unhappy or empty relationship and the desire to move on.

BARBARA *'I had been thinking of splitting up for a very long time. I realised that nothing whatever was going to either change or improve the existing useless relationship. My husband seemed determined to drink and smoke himself to death. He had also become involved in an incredibly hopeless relationship with one of his college students.'*

GRACE *'My husband left me with the words, "You're a wife in a million but I need a change." I felt like the whole world fell apart. For a long time I would not believe it could happen to us. I suppose I ran around like a headless chicken trying to make sense of it all.'*

CAROL *'Our marriage had been in a parlous state for eight years. I supposed we married the images of each other and the real thing came as an unpleasant shock to both of us. He thought I'd be a devoted wife – in other words, body servant, cook and silent recipient of his uncertain temper. I thought he was handsome, gentle and kind. He's still handsome.'*

You may not want to analyse your own relationship in great depth but it can be helpful to try to understand what has caused the strains in your marriage and what has brought you to contemplate separation or divorce. In the early stages of a marital breakdown it can be very difficult to step outside what is happening and take a cool, hard look at the circumstances that led to it. However, if you can do so, it may make it easier to come to terms with the situation you are in.

What's changed?

What is it that causes the cracks to appear? There are as many reasons as there are relationships. Some couples claim that the root of their discord is the sheer monotony of their marriage. They have slumped into a stupor from which neither party is prepared to stir until one of them acts upon their desire to escape. Perhaps there was a temporary cement – children, other dependants, career – which has now crumbled away. Others realise in retrospect that their marriage was doomed from the start through incompatibility, lack of love or unwillingness to recognise the true nature of the personalities involved. For many more there is a 'final straw' – the discovery of an affair, a last violent outburst, yet another unpaid bill.

The following are some of the 'change factors' that can put an intolerable strain on a marriage. The list is not exhaustive but it may help you to identify the issues you have had to confront within your own marriage and suggest ways in which they could have affected your relationship. Each by itself may not be sufficient to end a marriage; taken together or occurring over a long period of time, they may prove too tough a challenge. It might be worth considering the following points not just from your own perspective, but from your husband's too.

Changes relating to work, lifestyle and money

Career moves and promotions

- isolation and a sense of being uprooted for the non-career spouse;
- a sense of failure or unwillingness to 'perform' as a corporate husband or wife;
- resentment at one spouse's job taking precedence over the other's or the presumption that it should;
- resentment over a reversal in earning power and influence.

Redundancy

- social and financial pressure;
- upsetting of the daily routine;
- a devastating effect on morale which can affect communication and sexual relations;
- the need to question and rethink existing assumptions about who brings in money, spending power, and so on.

Retirement

- disappointment that retirement doesn't bring 'togetherness' or freedom;
- a devastating effect on the one who has retired, who suddenly doesn't know how to fill their days;
- upset that the normal routine is disrupted;
- resentment on the part of a husband whose wife continues to work and who appears to leave him to his own devices;

- resentment on the part of a non-working wife who finds her husband at home all day and making demands.

Changing fortunes

- desire for economic independence – usually felt by the non-'breadwinner';
- desire by one spouse to take control of financial matters – however dire;
- one spouse's resentment over the other's perceived meanness with money.

Lifestyle changes

- resentment or fear about downgrading or upgrading of their lifestyle;
- different and incompatible expectations;
- the perception that one spouse is a 'social failure' and is keeping the other one down;
- one spouse blaming the other for change – especially for the downgrading of their lifestyle.

Changes relating to recognition, attraction and sex

Lack of recognition

- anger or frustration at being invisible as a homemaker, worker or lover;
- resentment at being taken for granted;
- a need to seek and respond to recognition given by other people;
- abuse or humiliation.

JENNY *'My husband showed little interest in me and the children. We had no social life – he just fell asleep in his chair in the evening. I'd often wanted to leave him because he was old and unwell. The final push came* *when I started an affair with an ex-boyfriend. It helped give me the necessary confidence and showed me that life and sex could be fun!'*

MABEL *'My husband was a heavy drinker and a bully. He told me ten years before we separated that he had lost interest in me and intended to lead his own life henceforward. At this point I should have been screaming for help. Instead I did a cover-up job.'*

Diminishing attraction

- a realisation that you no longer find your spouse attractive as a personality or sexually;
- the discovery that others find you attractive even if your spouse doesn't;
- a need to 'prove' that attraction and secure the attentions of the opposite sex.

Sex and fidelity

- dissatisfaction of one partner with the other's changing sexual desires;
- a realisation that the other's sexual demands are intolerable;
- search outside the marriage for sexual satisfaction;
- the discovery of infidelity or realisation that an affair is not merely 'a fling'.

ALICE *'A friend of mine – as I thought – phoned me just after midnight to tell me that it was she my husband loved. It then transpired that they were having an affair. I was completely shattered – numbed and quite unable to formulate any positive ideas. I think my husband's affair was a symptom of his dissatisfaction with the marriage rather than the cause of it. Some time before my husband had said that he wanted to go and live alone – to "find out who I am". To my undying shame, I didn't follow this up but repressed it instead.'*

Changes relating to growing older, health and disability

Growing older

- frustration at growing older, which is exacerbated by the marriage;
- resentment that your spouse appears to be much older in looks and attitudes than you;
- a desire to be young again and take on the trappings of a youthful lifestyle;
- a desire to escape 'before it's too late'.

HEATHER *'Looking back I don't know how I stood it for so long. You know you've got to do something when you go on holiday without your husband and don't want to come home.'*

Children growing up

- achieving a 'marriage deadline', having decided to stay together until the children have left home;
- realisation that now the children have gone, there is nothing left to cement your relationship;
- encouragement by your children to leave the relationship;
- a desire to recreate for yourself happiness that your children have found in their own relationships.

Health

- resentment of the impact of your spouse's illness or disability;
- the end of willingness to tolerate psychological problems;
- the end of willingness to tolerate alcohol or drug problems.

Looking after yourself

There's no point in pretending that ending a marriage, particularly one of many years, is going to be easy. Breaking up is hard to do. It's a time of emotional turmoil and tough decisions.

At this moment, you may well be feeling overwhelmed by all that you are confronted with. Your emotions are probably running riot: one minute you find yourself in the blackest hole, the next you see light at the end of the tunnel. If there is any common experience to separation and divorce, it is this constant churning over of emotions. Ending a marriage is like bereavement and it is right to expect to mourn.

GRACE *'I found it very difficult to tell people. I felt intense shame. I had always told others I had the best husband in the world. I found remarks like "You will be laughing about it in a year's time" only made me feel that there was something wrong with me grieving the way I did.'*

CAROL *'Both my husband and I, despite disliking each other for years, went through a time of bereavement when we divorced. We both felt uprooted, even though we hadn't liked the flower bed. Odd isn't it?'*

Regardless of who instigated the separation, and whether it's amicable or acrimonious, the whole process will test you and make tremendous demands on you. It can be a period of great introspection and self-doubt. Yet it can also be a liberating experience and a time of great self-discovery.

YVONNE *'When my husband announced he wanted a divorce, I knew it was serious. In the past it had been me who had discussed the idea rather vaguely. I had a mixture of feelings. I was terrified of the future for myself, I thought it would mean being poor and lonely. But I was also relieved that a new life was about to start after the dreadful previous two years of unresolved tension.'*

JACQUI *'After a year or two of deteriorating communication between us, my husband suddenly left, leaving a note on the table. I was deeply shocked and frightened. I felt panicky, shaken, very tearful and then angry.*

As the weeks went by my feelings went from self-pity to self-blame to anger at his unexpected action – all in turn, several times a day.'

The following pages give you some ideas and advice on how to help yourself stay positive and manage the business of separation and divorce rather than let it manage you.

Taking time for yourself

First of all, take a little time to get yourself in perspective – the good and the bad. The following is definitely a 'take time out' exercise. Feel free to boast, to cry, to laugh, to make extravagant statements. Put down whatever comes into your head. There are no right or wrong answers. Keep what you have written. There may be blank spaces which you will one day fill. Your responses may rekindle ambitions, remind you that there are things that you enjoy in life, confirm that whatever you feel about yourself right now, you have talents. Hold on to your dreams and the 'feel good' sensations they produce. They will help keep you going through the dark moments.

About you – write down your favourite

Place	Film or theatre
Season	Radio or TV programme
Time of day	Food
Colour	Person
Book	Pastime
Piece of music	

Feelings of the moment

- The two things that make me feel most angry right now are . . .
- The two things that make me feel most frustrated are . . .
- The two things that I most fear are . . .
- The two things that hurt me most are . . .
- The two things that make me laugh most are . . .
- The two things that make me most happy right now are . . .

Expressing your emotions

- When I feel angry I . . .
- When I feel frustrated I . . .
- When I'm happy I . . .
- When I feel full of energy I . . .
- When I'm nervous I . . .

Body and soul

- The three things I most like about myself are . . .
- The three things I most dislike about myself are . . .
- My two best physical attributes are . . .
- My two worst physical attributes are . . .
- The three things I'm most proud of having achieved are . . .
- The three things I feel most frustrated or disappointed with myself for not having done are . . .

Dreams

- My greatest ambition is . . .
- Describe your idea of a 'perfect day'. Imagine where you would go, what you would do, what you would eat, how you would dress, what the weather would be like, whether you'd be alone or with a chosen person. Write down how you feel.
- Describe your dream home. Imagine the location, the number of rooms and layout, the furnishings and decor, who lives there with you. Write down how you feel.
- Describe your dream holiday. Imagine the scenery and the weather. Shut your eyes and feel what it's like to lie on a warm sandy beach or walk across a flower-strewn hillside or ski down a crisp snowy slope. Write down how you feel.
- Imagine you have at your disposal a top fashion designer, hair stylist and beautician to give you a total 'make over'. What would you ask them to do? How would you feel when they finish?

The future

- Next week I want to . . .
- Next month I want to . . .
- Next year I want to . . .
- In the next five years I want to . . .

Thinking positively

Inside each of our heads is a small voice. It is both our most loyal ally and our greatest critic. As an ally it can be the first to buck us up. Unfortunately we all too often dismiss its words of encouragement. As a critic it can be devastating, delivering huge blows to our self-confidence and dishing out big servings of guilt and self-doubt.

JACQUI *'As soon as I found out he had gone, all my confidence drained away and I felt terrible in every respect – appearance, professional and social skills. I blamed myself for the breakup and began to see all the preceding years of my life as a well-camouflaged failure.'*

ALICE *'The anguish was, and sometimes still is, extreme. The worst aspect of it was that I kept seeing myself through his eyes – as someone he didn't want anything more to do with. Therefore because I still loved him I thought of myself as someone pretty worthless in every possible way.'*

Take a simple everyday incident like the last time you stood in front of the mirror deciding what to wear.

YOU I think I'll wear my black suit.

SMALL VOICE *Not again, you look like an old crow.*

YOU OK, how about the floral dress?

SMALL VOICE *Bit extravagant isn't it. You're not exactly going to Buckingham Palace.*

YOU Well, all right then. What do you think of this knitted dress and jacket?

SMALL VOICE *Now that's better.*

You Oh, I don't know. Are you sure my bottom doesn't stick out?

Small voice *Only a tiny bit. It looks great, the colour shows off your eyes. Wear it.*

There's a dialogue going on inside everyone's head all the time. It's a perfectly healthy way of stopping to think before we open our mouths to say something or make a decision. It's a means of having a discussion when there's no one else around to talk things through with. The important thing is that you recognise whether your small voice is being constructive or whether it's trying to put you down.

Critic or ally?

Who talks most inside your head at the moment, ally or critic? And does its voice have a familiar ring about it?

The small voice as critic has a habit of saying things like: You've no right to do that. You'll only get it wrong. You mustn't. You shouldn't. What will people think? Everything is your fault. You've got no one to blame but yourself.

When you hear these things inside your head, do they sound like anyone you know? Your husband, for example, or one of your parents? A friend, schoolteacher or child?

Small voices like these can set you up to fail. They need challenging: Why haven't I the right to do this? Why should I get it wrong? And it's not the end of the world if I do. Why mustn't I? Why shouldn't I? Does it matter what people think? Why is everything my fault? I'm not responsible for everything that happens.

Equally your small voice can offer words of encouragement and challenge you when you are putting yourself down. Make an ally of your small voice. Use it to challenge moments of self-doubt. Listen to it and don't try to contradict it. Believe your small voice when it whispers you'll be OK: You can do it. Don't worry, you'll be fine. You can manage. You're not stupid. Don't be afraid. Take a deep breath and relax.

Jacqui *'I have begun to realise that it takes two to make a marriage go wrong and that I am worth more than I have been prepared to grant myself. I already feel more confident and believe that this change of circumstances should be viewed more as an opportunity than as a disaster. Now is the time for me to truly "be me" rather than half of something else.'*

Yvonne *'I remember looking at myself naked in the mirror and thinking, what man is ever going to desire me again? I thought my sex life was over. I was bucked up when a reasonably attractive man asked me out. I had been asked out previously by an unattractive man but that just made me feel worse!'*

Help yourself

1 Think of a recent situation when you heard your small voice talking inside your head. Make a list of the things you heard it telling you (you may hear the same things every day of your life). Next to each one put a tick if you think it was positive and a cross if you think it was negative.

2 Go back to each statement you've marked with a cross and write a challenge beside it. For example:
Negative statement: You'll never manage on your own. You're hopeless with figures.
Challenge: Why shouldn't I manage? I've run a household for years. Maybe I won't get everything right, but I'll learn and I'll get through.

Sabrina *'I was shocked to the core by my destructiveness in breaking up the family unit. I genuinely regarded it as another tear to the fabric of society. It is quite fortunate that every time I lost sight of my reasons for taking such a dreadful step my husband would ring up or come storming round in one of his rages. I remember with gratitude several occasions when I was able to think, "That's all right then, I do remember why I went and it was the right thing to do."'*

Barbara *'When I separated after 36 years of marriage I felt great – relieved, sad, glad – all mixed up! My husband was very casual and completely indifferent.'*

VALERIE *'Some people tend to be more shocked when you get divorced later in life. They say, "Fancy divorcing after all these years" as though, having endured a marriage for so long, you really might as well put up with it for the rest of your life. Others are full of admiration for what they see as your courage and ability to cope.'*

GERALDINE *'I think people are curious about women who get divorced later in life, especially when they flourish and enjoy life.'*

2.
Considering your options

Having come to terms with the fact that your marriage has deterio-rated, you may have a great sense of purpose about where you are going. On the other hand, you may still be feeling your way towards your next step. This section of the book explains the different options open to you and the legal consequences of following any one of them. There is also a section on where to go for more advice and information and a questionnaire to help you plan your next move.

Separation

For many, separation is quite definitely the first step on the road to divorce. It is a practical way of beginning to disentangle your lives as a couple while the divorce moves through the legal process.

For other couples, separation is a matter of gaining some breathing space. It enables you to step back from your relationship and look at ways to mend what you perceive as the holes in your marriage. You may use the opportunity to seek some counselling and to work at reconciling your differences. You may emerge from the separation experience with a stronger commitment to the marriage. Equally your time apart may bring recognition that there is no longer suffi-cient to sustain the relationship.

If the purpose of the separation is to provide a breathing space then it may be useful to set some kind of timetable for yourselves and be quite definite about what steps you will take towards reconciliation. If you get used to living apart and develop quite separate lives, it can become more difficult to reconcile your marriage – especially if one partner finds they enjoy living without their spouse.

For some, however, separation is a sort of limbo land. It is very clear that you can no longer go on living together but nor are you ready to contemplate the finality of divorce. You may exist in such a state for years.

WENDY *'My husband and I lived apart for a number of years. He met another woman and was in a hurry to divorce me but that relationship broke up very quickly. I had said I would do all the paperwork but I didn't proceed with the divorce because my work situation was very insecure and I didn't have the energy to do it. A couple of years later I felt I had finally got over my husband's love triangle and I had no regrets about seeking a divorce. Applying for the decree absolute was the ultimate statement that I was finally free.'*

JACQUI *'I agreed the marriage was in the doldrums but I thought it could be resuscitated. I tried to save the marriage first by seeing him as often as possible and asking him to come back – I didn't beg. After two years' separation he agreed that there might be grounds for a new life together. I joined him for a fortnight's holiday but it was hopeless and I came home half way through the planned time. I realised he was no longer the person I had married and he was determined to bring matters to an end – a conclusion which I shared.'*

There is no predetermined way to separate. It may be a well-thought through plan with a timetable – a case of waiting until one spouse has found a new home and then moving out more or less lock, stock and barrel. Or it may be a far more gradual process – gently slipping out of the marital home a suitcase at a time.

Separation in itself can be a far greater emotional upheaval than the granting of the final divorce decree. For many people it is the first really tangible recognition that the marriage is over or that they are facing serious problems as a couple. Equally important, a couple physically moving apart may be the first public signal that there are difficulties.

For increasing numbers of couples, however, financial and other constraints mean that they cannot physically move away from each other no matter how much their relationship has deteriorated. Attempting to live separate and contained lives in these circumstances brings additional stresses and strains.

Whatever the circumstances of the separation – whether it is the logical conclusion of years of a deteriorating relationship or a spur of the moment decision; whether it's short-term, a permanent prospect or a fill-in until the divorce – you ought to consider your legal and financial position (see p 26).

Things to think about

- Are you clear about why you are separating? Is it to help you find ways to learn to live together again? Or is it to see how you each fare on your own?

- Are you and your husband separating for the same reasons? For example, is he living apart from you because he wants to start afresh, while you are hoping that time away will bring you together again?

- Are you separating simply to put off getting divorced? Separation can enable you to cling on to a relationship which is in fact completely over. Sometimes it is more positive to make the final break than to drift on with uncertain status.

- If you have no immediate plans for divorce, who will have financial responsibility for the matrimonial home? How will you find the resources to run two households? What about finding accommodation for the spouse who moves out?

HEATHER *'I was terrified but absolutely resolute about the separation. How do you tell your husband – who's kidding himself that nothing's wrong – that you're deserting him, knowing that he doesn't have the personal or* *family resources to cope with the situation? Especially when you've been married for 25 years and he refuses to believe a word you are telling him. After the death of my father it was the most traumatic thing in my life.'*

FRANCES *'Over 13 years my husband formed a liaison with another woman. Perhaps through fear, insecurity or whatever I never had sufficient courage to finish the marriage. I always nurtured the idea that it was salvageable. Each time I said I wanted a divorce he said we should stay together. I used to feel panic at the thought even though I was independent of him financially. I know now I should have divorced him but the seed of hope took a long time to die.'*

The legal issues

At its most simple, separation can mean a husband and wife choosing to live apart on an informal basis for a matter of days or weeks, dealing with financial and other matters on an ad hoc basis. In fact there is no need to take any legal steps at all when you separate, providing you trust each other and can agree between you about financial matters and arrangements for any dependent children.

However, even if your relationship is very amicable, it is advisable to begin to address and formalise the financial aspects of your lives. You can do this in the form of a separation agreement. Once again, this can be a very basic document written by your husband and yourself, or you can ask your solicitor to draw one up. If you want to make your arrangements more formal you can go to court. Separation agreements are explained in detail on pages 88–89.

If your relationship is very difficult when you separate and you cannot agree about financial and other matters, then you should seek the help of a solicitor or go to court. It doesn't matter whether or not you intend to get divorced, you can apply for financial support (known as financial relief) through the court (see pp 89–90). The court can always be asked to intervene when a husband and wife are in dispute. Maintenance for children can be dealt with through the Child Support Agency. Going to court will not rule out a reconciliation. However, if you have no alternative but to go to court, that is obviously an indication of the state of the marriage, and going to court is not likely to enhance your prospects of getting back together.

Judicial separation

Judicial separation is rarely used these days. It is a means of legally recognising separation for couples who are unable or unwilling to get divorced, perhaps for religious or emotional reasons.

Judicial separation is a court procedure and you will therefore need to fulfil certain criteria, similar to those for getting divorced. The fundamental difference between judicial separation and divorce is that the former will not enable you to remarry. While it gives legal and financial protection to separated spouses, it is possible to obtain similar protection through the court without going through a judicial separation.

If divorce remains an option, then it is not usually worth the expense of pursuing a judicial separation. If, having got such a separation, you later decide to petition for divorce, you will need to start from the beginning like everyone else.

Divorce

Divorce is the ultimate legal severing of a marriage. The actual procedure is relatively straightforward and can be completed quite simply. What tend to complicate matters are all the other issues that get thrown into the breakup pot – finances, your home, your children.

Some women find the process of divorce tremendously liberating. It may be the first time you have taken real control of your life, certainly in your relationship. Divorce inevitably forces people to take a lot of critical decisions, make compromises and take a hard look at themselves. What strikes many women is the startling finality of the decree absolute. No matter how long the process has taken, no matter what the circumstances, you may still feel a sense of complete disbelief at the end of it.

Once you start proceedings, it can become something of a roller coaster towards the final divorce decree. For this reason, it's important to have thought through, first of all, whether divorce is really what you want, and second, if you do go through with the divorce, what you want out of it.

FRANCES *'I think you need to weigh up the pros and cons of divorce very carefully. Divorce is not an easy road. Don't be rushed into it. Explore every avenue. Have counselling. Take your time. Make no rash moves. If the quality of your life is paramount and he is destroying you then leave him. If, despite it all, things aren't that bad, then stay and find a lover!'*

VALERIE *'Think long and hard about whether you enjoy or detest solitude. Take advice on your finances. Don't be afraid of asking for help from children and friends. Have as many interests as possible. If you need a man in your life, prepare for this being the most difficult aspect of all.'*

EUNICE *'After years of misery and loneliness, deciding to go ahead with the divorce gave me a great sense of relief.'*

Things to think about

- Are you clear in your own mind that the marriage has broken down completely and cannot be revived? There is little point in starting proceedings – and incurring the expense of doing so – if in fact you want to see if you can reconcile the relationship.

- Is divorce being used – by either of you – as a threat or does it reflect the state of your marriage?

- The divorce procedure itself is a cold and calculated legal process. Have you found someone or something other than lawyers or the legal system upon which to vent your anger/fear/frustrations about your life at this moment?

- Have you thought about where you will live and what you will live on after you and your husband part company? These will probably have a much greater impact on your life than the tearing up of a marriage certificate.

- Divorce – and separation – can take an enormous amount of energy and commitment, especially if negotiations become difficult. Think about your own resources and sources of support.

The legal issues

Divorce involves a strictly regulated legal procedure. You will need to satisfy certain criteria before you get divorced and you will need to adhere to a set legal process, as explained in detail in Chapter 3. Once you have your final divorce decree, you will be free to remarry. Equally, the divorce is final and there is no going back on your previous relationship. If you reconcile with your former husband, you will have to remarry.

Annulment

This isn't an option for most people. A marriage can be annulled only in very specific circumstances. The effect of a decree of nullity is to treat the marriage as if it had never taken place in law. However, any children remain legitimate.

In order to have your marriage annulled you will have to prove one of two things: either that the marriage is void – never legally existed (this could be because one of the partners was already married) – or that the marriage was legal but is voidable, for example because it has never been consummated.

If you wish to have your marriage annulled because you believe it is voidable, then you will need to start proceedings within three years of your marriage except if it has not been consummated. You should always seek the advice of a solicitor in this situation.

Staying together

The fact that you have contemplated separation or divorce – or even begun to take steps towards one or the other – does not mean that you have to go through with either. Even doing something very practical, like consulting a solicitor or moving out of your home, may be a sign of your total frustration with the state of your marriage or a cry for help rather than a definite desire to end the relationship. Consulting a solicitor or completing a divorce petition may make your spouse realise just how serious you are about the problems in the marriage and may spur him on to try to resolve them.

The important thing to remember is that what matters is that you exercise choice. Feeling obliged to go ahead with a divorce is just as powerless as feeling obliged to remain in a destructive or unfulfilling relationship.

Choice is often linked to a sense of control. However, few of us ever have the opportunity to choose exactly what we wish and therefore to exercise complete control. Most of life is a compromise, especially when it comes to relationships.

If you decide to remain with your husband it's up to you to make up your own mind on what terms you will stay together and whether you are prepared to continue indefinitely with the relationship if nothing changes.

RUTH *'I felt it would be a terrible thing to be divorced twice and that I ought to try harder to make it work. I think what really stopped me being honest with myself was the idea that I needed to try harder, that it must be my fault. If I loved him more, he'd change. If I became a nicer person, he'd treat me better. Nice people have successful marriages – therefore I must be a failure, no good, horrible. I also felt very seriously that marriage was for ever and had always thought that the nicest thing in the world would be to have a happy family life.'*

PAM *'I didn't know the extent of the relationship he was then involved in. All the while I really loved him even though I felt I was trapped in a bug* *hole waiting for him to dig me out. Looking back it seems ridiculous to think that anything could have improved.'*

Things to think about

- Does your husband know how you feel? Is this something you are going to be able to work through as a couple?

- If your relationship remains the same, will you continue to live with your husband? Unless you are prepared to go on living in the same unfulfilling marriage indefinitely, it may be worth setting a deadline for yourself. What do you want to change and what steps will you take to achieve those changes? What will you do if after a certain time things remain the same?

- Are you staying together because it's what you want or because you feel you have no other option? Do you prefer to remain with the life you know – with all its attendant frustrations – rather than risk the unknown?

- Are you staying together for religious reasons, because of social pressures or for the sake of your children? Are these reasons justified?

- Do you really believe you can change your relationship or is it only a very vague hope?

Where to go for advice and professional help

However amicable the ending of a marriage, separation and divorce hurt – emotionally and financially. It can be difficult to remain cool and detached throughout what is a very personal and often painful process. There are, however, a number of different organisations – counselling, mediation and legal – that can help you confront the difficulties in your relationship and manage the separation and divorce process constructively.

An acrimonious breakup can have a huge impact, not just on you and your husband but on your children, the extended family and any future relationships. In the long term there is absolutely nothing to be gained by being obstructive, manipulative or vindictive. In the short term all you will achieve are mounting legal costs and a tremendous strain on your mental and physical well-being. It is in everybody's interests to make the process of splitting up as businesslike and civilised as possible.

The next section looks at three sources of professional advice and support:

- marriage guidance and counselling;
- conciliation and mediation services;
- solicitors.

Marriage guidance and counselling

The best-known provider of marriage guidance and counselling services is Relate (formerly the Marriage Guidance Council) or London Marriage Guidance (addresses on p 154). However, there are many other smaller organisations which provide a range of counselling opportunities for individuals and families (addresses on pp 153–154). Many religious groups have specific counselling organisations. Your doctor may also be able to put you in touch with a counsellor. Some surgeries now have therapists attached to the practice.

You do not need to be on the verge of divorce to seek help. In fact the earlier you go the better. Organisations like Relate can support you in a variety of ways, from relationship counselling to divorce counselling and conciliation (see below). They aim to help couples understand the cause of their problems and enrich their relationships. However, they won't try to make you stay together, nor will a good counsellor tell you what you should do. Although it's obviously much better if both you and your husband can attend counselling sessions, if your husband is unwilling to go along you should go by yourself. Counsellors are used to working with one partner alone.

Relate also has therapists who work with couples who are facing specifically sexual problems. Again, if you think that this may be at the root of your marital difficulties your doctor may be able to refer you to a counsellor.

Many of the counselling organisations offer free services to those who cannot afford to pay for them. However, if you are earning you will be expected to contribute something. You should always make sure that you know how much each session is going to cost you and how many sessions your counsellor thinks you will need.

GERALDINE *'Two years after we separated we agreed to go to Relate to decide where our relationship was and what we wanted to do for the future. I felt very strongly that I wanted to work on the many positives in order to see if we could continue as a couple. My husband was very unsure. Eventually I suggested to him that in every way other than in actual words he was telling me that the marriage was over. He didn't disagree. I felt greatly relieved that after two years of uncertainty a conclusion had been reached.'*

Conciliation and mediation services

These should not be confused with the reconciliation services described above. Unlike organisations such as Relate, the aim of conciliation and mediation is not to explore why the marriage has broken down or to encourage you to reconcile your relationship. These services aim to help you manage the separation and divorce process in the most positive and constructive way. The two terms are often used interchangeably, but mediation is probably the more popular term.

Mediation services offer a neutral meeting place in which you and your husband can discuss financial issues and arrangements for your children with an independent person. The aim is to enable you to reach decisions between yourselves without the need to involve solicitors and courts. By going to an independent mediation service you can take some of the tension out of your discussions and use the practical experience of a third party.

Most mediation services are coordinated by National Family Mediation (formerly the National Family Conciliation Council address on p 153). You can contact them directly or ask your local Citizens Advice Bureau about services in your area. The cost of the sessions varies but the underlying principle is that mediation should be available to everyone regardless of income.

You can go along to a mediator at any point in the separation and divorce procedure. Obviously the earlier you go the more benefit you will derive. Although in theory mediation does away with the need to use a solicitor, you should always seek professional advice about any proposed financial settlement.

Solicitors

Finding the right solicitor can make all the difference to the separation and divorce experience. So how can you ensure that your solicitor will be the best one for you and that you get the most from your legal adviser?

Until your divorce is over and every last loose end tied up, you won't know for certain that the solicitor you consulted has been effective. However, you can increase your chances of success considerably by following these simple guidelines:

- Choose someone who specialises in matrimonial and family work. The solicitor who looked after your house purchase or drew up your Will so well is unlikely to be the best person to handle your divorce. You can get the name of a suitable solicitor by contacting the Solicitors' Family Law Association (address on p 155). The Association sets out a code of practice for its members. Its aim is to resolve cases with the least disruption to the family and without drawing the process out unnecessarily. The approach is constructive and conciliatory rather than aggressive and antagonistic.

- Go to your meetings well prepared; make a list of the points you want to discuss and take along copies of any relevant documents. Turn up on time for your appointments.

- Don't use your solicitor as a counsellor, companion, shoulder to cry on or emotional punch bag: you will pay for the privilege and you probably won't get very good advice either.

- Be persistent but patient. Remember that negotiations take time, especially if your relationship with your husband is somewhat fraught. Delays aren't always the fault of your own solicitor. There may be bureaucratic hold-ups or your husband's solicitors may drag their heels. Solicitors who practise on their own can sometimes be overwhelmed by work.

- Make sure that your solicitor explains what is happening in simple English, keeps you up to date, responds to your enquiries promptly, and supplies you with drafts of important letters and copies of correspondence.

- If you have a problem with your solicitor then talk to them about it. Explain clearly why you are dissatisfied and what you would like done to remedy the situation. Give them the opportunity to put their side or apologise.

- Finally, remember it is your divorce and your life. Ask your solicitor for information and guidance, but ultimately it is up to you to make the decisions.

Solicitors' charges

Before you instruct a solicitor and ask them to act for you, you must establish how much they are going to charge. Solicitors basically charge by the hour. Every telephone call (made or answered), letter and meeting is accounted for, and they will all add up. You will need to establish how much your solicitor's hourly rate is and ask them to estimate how much the work you are asking them to do will cost. In addition you will need to establish the likely cost of disbursements – court fees and other expenses. Don't forget that VAT will be added to your final bill.

It's not unusual to be asked to pay a sum of money on account before your solicitor takes on your case. Many solicitors also present interim bills, which at least allows you to keep track of your expenses. In addition, many will accept regular monthly payments, which will lessen the burden of a large final bill.

If you feel you have been overcharged for your solicitor's services then you can challenge the bill. The Solicitors Complaints Bureau (address on p 155) produces a free leaflet called *Complaints about Solicitors' Charges*.

If you receive Legal Aid and the statutory charge applies (see p 48) then your solicitor must send you a very detailed bill. You have the right to object to any part of the bill and to request that the bill is assessed or 'taxed' through the court.

Don't forget, too, that your local Citizens Advice Bureau, advice centre or law centre may also be a valuable source of free information and advice.

For information about getting help with legal costs, see pages 47–50.

What's best for me?

You may have a very clear idea of what action you want to take or you may feel uncertain about your next move. The aim of this questionnaire is to help you to clarify your feelings and decide which path you should follow.

For each question tick the statement which best reflects your thoughts and mood at the moment.

Question 1

A I cannot see any future in our marriage.

B I don't think we can go on living together.

C I think we need some breathing space to sort ourselves out.

D Our marriage is very rocky but I don't believe it's over.

Question 2

A My husband says our marriage is over and I think he's right.

B I can no longer tolerate my husband's behaviour.

C I recognise that life has been particularly stressful but I believe we need the opportunity to work things through.

D We've always had our ups and downs but I think we've weathered most of the storms so far.

Question 3

A I'm not at all surprised at the idea that we might not be together any more. In fact I'm quite relieved.

B I feel a sense of loss that the marriage may be over. I need time to adjust and work out whether a permanent separation is right for us.

C I feel very strange about splitting up. Most of me wants the marriage to continue working.

D I'm completely shocked by the idea of our marriage breaking up. I can't believe that such a thing could happen.

Question 4

A I have found someone new and can see a different life ahead.

B I'm not the same woman my husband married. I have different expectations and ambitions now.

C I think that there's a lot still going for us. We need to step outside the relationship and see how we can help ourselves.

D I think that basically we are the same two people we were when we got married, we just need to rekindle that first love.

Question 5

A I feel quite liberated by the idea of being on my own in the future.

B I am sure that I will cope with being a single woman but I'm just not ready for that step at the moment.

C I still see myself as a married woman. I find it very difficult to think of myself being on my own.

D My whole identity is as half of a married partnership. I can't grasp the idea of being a single woman at all.

Question 6

A I want to get the legalities over and done with as soon as possible and get on with my life.

B I definitely don't think things can continue as they are but I'm not sure we are ready to tear up our marriage certificate.

C I feel very unsettled. The idea of ending our marriage for good seems a long way off. I feel there's a lot we can do before we get there.

D I want to look at the positive ways of making the marriage work.

Question 7

A Divorce can be a very positive thing.

B Divorce is a fact of life but I don't think you should rush into it.

C You need to try out every other option before you embark on a divorce.

D Divorce is very much a last option. I think you have to work very hard at a marriage and stick it out.

If you tick mostly As

You appear to have made up your mind, or come to terms with the fact, that divorce is a foregone conclusion. It's worth recognising that however committed and positive you feel about the process of divorcing, you may still feel a sense of profound grief. As with most things, it's hard to keep your emotions on an even keel, so expect both the ups and the downs. You will now need to address some of the practical aspects of divorce such as finding a solicitor (if you decide to use one), completing the divorce petition and thinking about financial arrangements.

If you tick mostly Bs

You probably do not feel ready yet to commit yourself to the finality of divorce, although it may be something that you accept will eventually happen. You are most likely to be currently living apart from your husband or contemplating separation. Separation will give you some breathing space to decide where you want to go next and at what pace. Unless you envisage living apart for only a very short while you may want to think about drawing up a suitable separation agreement and addressing some of the important financial issues.

If you tick mostly Cs

You have very mixed emotions about the whole business of separation and divorce. You are probably not ready for divorce just yet and even separation might be difficult to contemplate. However, you recognise that you have problems with your relationship. You may want to seek counselling from an organisation such as Relate to see if you can find a way to reconcile your marriage. You may also want personal counselling to help you come to terms with what has happened and explore whether or not you should continue to put energy into your existing relationship. A period of separation may be worth considering to give you and your husband the space to think about how to resolve some of your difficulties.

If you tick mostly Ds

You appear very fearful about divorce and separation. It may be that there is plenty left in your relationship and that it is worth working hard to reconcile your differences. On the other hand, you may simply not want to face up to the fact that your marriage has broken down and cannot be salvaged. If you are in this situation it is important that you seek expert counselling to help you work through your feelings. This should help you determine whether there is real hope for your relationship. If it is indeed over, then you ought to put your energies into making sure that you are prepared — financially, if perhaps not yet emotionally — to deal with the future.

DORA *'Looking back it seems as if it happened to a different person. My husband was a gambler and a charmer. It was leaving, then pleading, then coming back. I tried to save the marriage. It seemed we couldn't live together and we couldn't live without each other. Even now it wouldn't surprise him if I turned up at his door. My ex's behaviour, the way I put up with it, it all seems now to be mad.'*

EUNICE *'My biggest concern was how we were going to live out the last months together with as little acrimony as possible. The wait while our lawyers sorted things out was hell as I tried to keep a civilised life going for us all. I just took one day at a time and one thing at a time.'*

VALERIE *'My husband found out I was having an affair and told me to stop. I refused and he said he would divorce me. I think it was a bluff meant to frighten me into submission. In fact I was both surprised and delighted as I had been wanting an end to the marriage for years.'*

3.
The legal breakup

The actual business of getting divorced consists of a number of procedures: the legal procedures of ending the marriage and making arrangements for the care of the children and the financial procedures – sorting out the future of the matrimonial home and making arrangements for day-to-day money, pensions and so on. Some will be simple and quite straightforward to sort out. A few will need greater strategic negotiations and may require professional help or the intervention of the court. You will not get your final divorce decree until you have at least completed all the legal procedures to the satisfaction of the court.

Before you make the first practical move towards putting the divorce process in motion – whether by visiting a solicitor or obtaining a blank copy of the divorce petition – you need to do some preparation:

1 You must ensure that you meet the legal requirements to entitle you to divorce (see below).

2 You should consider how you are going to pay for it.

The divorce who's who

The petitioner The spouse seeking the divorce who completes the divorce application form (the divorce petition).

The respondent The other spouse, whom the petitioner wishes to divorce.

Co-respondent In cases of adultery, this is the person with whom the respondent has had a sexual relationship.

The parties This refers to both the petitioner and the respondent and, where appropriate, the co-respondent.

Decree A court order.

Since most divorce cases are initiated by women, it is assumed in this chapter that the petitioner will be you, the woman.

Meeting the legal requirements

In order to obtain a divorce you will need to prove four things.

1 Your marriage is valid

In most cases an official copy – not a photocopy – of your marriage certificate will do. If the marriage took place outside England or Wales, it may be necessary to produce other evidence and an officially certified or sworn translation of the foreign marriage document.

If you do not have a copy of your marriage certificate you can get one by applying by post to the Registrar General of Births, Deaths and Marriages (look in the telephone directory under 'Registration of Births, Deaths and Marriages'). You will need to send a cheque or postal order for £15 (1995 price) made out to HM Paymaster General. Alternatively you can call into the Office of Population Censuses and Surveys in London (address on p 155). They will charge you £5.50, and they do not accept applications by post. In both cases you should give details of the date and place of your marriage and your and your husband's full names.

2 You have been married for at least one year

You cannot get divorced if you have been married for less than a year.

3 You satisfy the residence qualifications

You or your husband must have your permanent home in England or Wales when the divorce petition is started. This is known as being legally domiciled in this country. You will also qualify if either of you has been living in the country for at least a year before the petition is begun. If you are not sure whether you are legally domiciled, or have any query over your immigration status, you must seek the advice of a solicitor.

4 Your marriage has irretrievably broken down

There is only one ground for divorce: that the marriage has irretrievably broken down. In other words, it is over for good. In order to prove this you will have to show one of the following 'facts'.

Adultery

Not only must your husband, the respondent, have committed adultery but also you, the petitioner, must find it intolerable to go on living with him. (You cannot base your divorce petition on your own adultery.)

A relationship that does not actually involve sexual intercourse is not adultery – although it may constitute unreasonable behaviour (see below). If a wife is accused of adultery, then the alleged sexual intercourse must be voluntary. A woman who is raped has not committed adultery.

If you continue to live with your husband 'as man and wife' for more than six months after you have proof (not just suspicions) of his adultery, then it will be taken that you have accepted his behaviour and you will not be able to divorce on grounds of adultery. However, if your husband later resumes his affair or commits adultery with a new partner then you are entitled to petition for divorce on the basis of his recent adultery – providing you do not continue to live with him 'as man and wife'.

Providing the respondent does not contest the claim of adultery, this is often the quickest and simplest ground for securing a divorce. However, if your husband refuses to admit the adultery and you have no hard evidence that it has happened, he may contest the divorce and this could become extremely expensive. In this situation you would be far better off finding another ground on which to base the divorce. Bear in mind, however, that he may equally contest a claim of unreasonable behaviour.

Unreasonable behaviour

This means that your husband has behaved in such a way that you can no longer be expected to live with him.

Unreasonable behaviour is difficult to categorise but it includes violence; alcoholism or drug addiction; obsessive behaviour; insanity; mental cruelty, taunting and public humiliation; excessive demands for, or refusal of, sex; meanness with money. Incompatibility or basic personality clashes will not count as unreasonable behaviour – unless of course one partner has, for example, become abusive, withdrawn all affection, or caused the other to leave the home.

Once again, you will need to show that you have not lived with your husband 'as man and wife' for more than six months after the last act of unreasonable behaviour referred to in the divorce petition.

Unreasonable behaviour can sometimes be difficult to prove. If you are in any doubt, seek the advice of a solicitor.

Desertion

This means that your husband left you, against your will, two years ago or more. If your husband can prove that he made a genuine and realistic offer to return home to you, then the 'desertion' will not be allowed as proof that the marriage has broken down irretrievably.

NOTE A wife will not be regarded as having deserted her husband if she leaves him because of his violence towards her. The same would apply to a man in a similar situation.

Two years' separation with consent

You and your husband must have lived apart for at least two years and your husband must agree to the divorce.

You may have to postpone your divorce if you and your husband reconcile after an initial separation. So long as the time you live together again is less than six months in total (even if that time is divided over a number of years) then you can continue with the divorce. However, you will have to add the time you spend together as a couple on to the separation period.

If you live together again for more than six months in total – for example, for three months in the first year and for two three-month periods in the second – then you will have to find another ground on which to prove that the marriage has broken down. Or you can start the two-year separation period over again.

Five years' separation without consent

This means that you and your husband have lived apart for a continuous period of five years. Your husband will not have to give his consent. If you and your husband reconcile for a period after the initial separation, the same rules apply as with two-year separations, described above.

It is virtually impossible to stop a divorce going through after five years' separation. If you find yourself on the receiving end, then you may be able to delay the divorce for financial reasons but you will not be able to put it off for ever (see pp 69–70). In this situation you must see a solicitor.

Meeting the costs of divorce

Divorce need not be an expensive exercise. An uncomplicated break, where both husband and wife agree about dividing the family finances and arrangements for any dependent children, need involve only the minimum of expense. You will have the standard court fees for the divorce itself, and perhaps the costs involved in getting a duplicate marriage certificate.

At the other end of the scale, where a couple cannot agree about anything – the divorce is contested, there are huge arguments about money, and there is no agreement over the children – a divorce can result in legal bills running into many thousands of pounds.

No one really 'wins' in these cases. The important thing to remember is that whatever you spend between you in seeing the divorce through will ultimately come out of your joint family wealth. This applies even if one of you is getting State help to pay for your legal advice (see below).

This is not to say that you should give in on all counts and not 'fight your corner'. An effective solicitor will know how to negotiate – when to stick to their guns and when to concede. A family mediator or conciliator may help you achieve much the same thing (see pp 33–34). It is possible to come out with a good deal without spilling the last drop of blood, if indeed spilling any at all. There is absolutely no point in creating a battlefield: such an exercise will cost you both dearly.

RUTH *'To me it is extremely important to find a solicitor who you "feel" right with. My solicitor always listened to me with attention and respect – an enormous help in restoring my dignity and self-esteem. He made me feel as if my opinion really mattered. I felt very nervous in court but I felt secure with my solicitor. It's worth working up your self-esteem at a time like this. Write down a list of things you really like about yourself before you have to face the formality of the court. Take along a friend who will support and encourage you and maybe even offer some light relief* *afterwards. I have found my friends enormously willing to help me when I ask them.'*

Yvonne *'I went to see a solicitor immediately after we agreed to separate. But it was far too soon. I was in too much of an emotional turmoil and there was no urgent need to sort out practical matters. Later I went to see another solicitor but I found the adversarial approach quite unnecessary and offputting, so I let matters drop. When eventually I petitioned for divorce after two years I did it myself without using a solicitor. Things were much less fraught emotionally and it was very matter of fact. I would recommend using this method wherever possible.'*

Can I get help with my legal costs?

If you have little or no money of your own, you may be entitled to some help with the cost of legal fees. As far as matrimonial cases are concerned there are two types of scheme:

- the legal advice and assistance scheme – commonly known as the Green Form Scheme;
- Legal Aid.

These are explained in more detail below.

Both these schemes are means-tested according to the amount of disposable income and savings or capital you have. Financial help is awarded on a sliding scale for Legal Aid. The Green Form Scheme is simply a case of qualify or not. Unless you have a substantial income or more than a couple of thousand pounds worth of capital, it is always worth asking your solicitor on your first visit if you qualify for help. Assets that are in dispute such as the matrimonial home do not count for the purposes of determining eligibility for help with legal costs.

Even if you are granted help, use your solicitor as effectively as if you were paying for their expertise out of your own pocket (see pp 34–35). The amount of time a solicitor can spend with you is limited under the Green Form Scheme (see below). In addition, you may have to make at least a contribution towards your legal costs.

At the end of the day the legal costs you incur will be set against any property or other assets 'recovered or preserved' for you when the divorce is settled. This is known as the statutory charge. In effect you may have to 'repay' your costs. However, there are exemptions and it is possible to postpone paying the statutory charge, but if you do so you will have to pay interest. Make sure you ask your solicitor to explain this to you fully.

If you apply for help with legal costs, only your own income, and not that of your husband, will be taken into account. This means that even if your husband is a high earner, if you earn nothing yourself (and have little or no capital) you can still get help.

If you receive Income Support, Family Credit or Disability Working Allowance then you should be entitled to assistance. However, you will also need to satisfy the savings criteria, and these vary according to the scheme.

NOTE Not all solicitors offer help under these schemes, so check before you make the appointment.

The Green Form Scheme

So called because the application form is green, this scheme covers you for initial advice and assistance from your solicitor and work on an uncontested divorce. Under the scheme, solicitors can provide advice on a wide range of matters such as:

- whether you have grounds for divorce or judicial separation;
- spousal maintenance and the family home;
- maintenance and arrangements for the children.

They can also help manage the divorce procedure for you and help you apply for further financial assistance.

The time you are allowed under the scheme is limited, but your solicitor can apply for an extension if they can prove that the extra work is merited. In addition, there may be circumstances where your solicitor could apply on a separate green form for assistance with other matters relating to the breakup of the marriage, for example correspondence with creditors or the building society.

Assistance by way of representation (ABWOR)

This covers the cost of a solicitor preparing your case and representing you in, for example, maintenance applications. Your solicitor will advise you if you need to make an application.

Legal Aid

Legal Aid covers you for the actual court proceedings. It's designed to cover more complex – and therefore usually more expensive – work. Legal Aid is usually needed where there is likely to be some kind of dispute or court hearing over, for example, financial settlements or arrangements for children.

However, Legal Aid is not automatically given even if you meet the financial criteria. The Legal Aid Board will also have to be satisfied that your case stands a reasonable chance of success and that it would be in the public interest to pursue it.

In addition, Legal Aid may not be granted immediately and it may take some weeks before a Legal Aid certificate is issued. However, you will get emergency Legal Aid if, for example, you are the victim of domestic violence and need an injunction to bar your husband from the house (see pp 75–77).

If you are entitled to help with your legal costs, it is best to be patient and not insist that your solicitor rushes ahead. If you do so you may find that you run up legal bills which fall between the ending of the Green Form Scheme and the issuing of your Legal Aid certificate. Be wary and check that whatever legal help you receive is covered by one or other of the schemes.

Don't be tempted to mislead the Legal Aid Board about your financial position. If they find you out, your Legal Aid certificate can be revoked. This means that your solicitor will then be entitled to recover their fees and any other costs from you; this will be done through the Legal Aid Board. In addition, by giving fraudulent information, you could risk imprisonment.

A step-by-step guide to the divorce procedure

Almost all divorces are undefended: this means that the respondent doesn't contest the divorce. Even if you cannot agree about the financial settlement or arrangements for the children, you can still proceed with an undefended divorce.

Most straightforward cases are dealt with by the Special Procedure. This means that all the paperwork is reviewed by the district judge and you never need set foot inside the court.

All divorces, regardless of whether the respondent intends to defend they, begin in the same way. Specific information about defended divorces can be found on pages 66–70.

The Lord Chancellor's Department produces an excellent set of leaflets explaining how the divorce procedure works. You can get free copies by contacting your local divorce county court.

NOTE You will not get Legal Aid in order to be represented in an undefended divorce – there should be no need for representation in any case. However, you can still apply under the Green Form Scheme (see pp 48–49) for help with completing the divorce petition and other forms. You can also apply for Legal Aid in order to be represented at hearings to do with the financial settlement or with arrangements for your children.

RUTH *'The most difficult thing about the actual process of divorce was getting myself to believe I could do it! My solicitor was helpful but I found the legal processes grind awfully slowly. Once I had made up my mind, I wanted it all to happen and to get on with the rest of my life.'*

GERALDINE *'I don't think you need a solicitor, the court process is simple. In dealing with lawyers I found it important to decide what I wanted and to state it to them assertively. Don't assume they're efficient – they can be as slapdash as anyone else!'*

Step 1 *Obtaining the application form*

You can get copies of the application form or petition free from your nearest divorce county court – look in your local telephone directory for their address, which will usually appear under 'Courts'. In addition, if you live in London, you could also go to the Principal Registry of the Family Division of the High Court. The courts are open from 10 am until 4 pm Monday to Friday. The Principal Registry is open until 4.30 pm. You can also get copies at a legal stationers or through a Citizens Advice Bureau.

You will need three copies of the divorce petition (form D8). One copy is for the court, one is for the court to send to your husband, and one is for you to keep (or you could just fill in two copies and make a photocopy for yourself). It may also be worth taking an extra copy or two just in case you make a mistake completing it.

If you are divorcing your husband on the ground of adultery and you are naming his partner, the co-respondent, on the petition, you will need to get an additional copy for the court to send to them. Naming co-respondents is generally discouraged unless there are exceptional reasons.

If you have dependent children you will also need three copies of the Statement of Arrangements for the Children (form D8A). Again, you may wish to ask for an extra copy. (For further information on children and divorce, see pp 121–137.)

Step 2 *Completing the divorce petition*

The petition is reasonably straightforward, and if you want to complete the form yourself you should be able to do so without too much difficulty. The form also contains information and guidance notes which you should read.

You will be known as the petitioner and your husband will be the respondent (see pp 41–42).

You will need to state on which of the five facts you have based the divorce (see pp 43–45), and on page 3, headed 'Particulars', you will need to give brief details to support the fact you have given as the basis for the divorce. Think carefully before you write – you need to be concise and logical but thorough. The guidance notes are worth reading.

Adultery

You don't have to give the name of the woman with whom your husband has committed adultery but you must state that you find it intolerable to go on living with him. If you know the name of the co-respondent (the person with whom your husband has committed adultery), you can include it along with her address. You are also asked to state where and when the adultery has taken place – if you know. If you don't have any of this information you can simply write, 'The respondent has committed adultery with a woman whose identity is unknown to the petitioner at addresses unknown between [date] and [date].'

If your husband does not admit to adultery and you cannot provide any hard evidence that it happened, he may contest the divorce and the costs could escalate. If this happens you would be far better off basing the divorce on another ground.

If you give the co-respondent's name and address then you will have to complete an extra petition form for the court to send to her.

Note A co-respondent does not need to admit the adultery for the divorce to go through, which is why there is little point in naming them in the first place.

Unreasonable behaviour

This is very difficult to define, as explained on page 44. The court will be looking for evidence that the respondent's behaviour is so intolerable that you can no longer be expected to carry on living with him.

You will usually need to show a pattern of unreasonable behaviour and cite a number of incidents. For example, if you feel you cannot tolerate your husband's abusive behaviour you might write something like: 'My husband is very abusive towards me. He humiliates me and swears at me in front of the children. He shouts in my face and has physically abused me. He also withholds housekeeping money from me.' You would then need to give specific examples with dates and times if you can. Try to list the examples in chronological order. It can be helpful to give details of the first, worst and most recent incidents. Do not exaggerate your claims, and keep the allegations to a minimum.

If the last incident of unreasonable behaviour took place more than six months ago but you are still living with your husband, you may be able to proceed with the divorce on this ground but you will need to submit a detailed and plausible explanation as to why you are still together.

If there has been one major incident that has caused you to petition for divorce – your husband attacked you, or you discovered he was having a homosexual affair – then obviously it will not be necessary to show a pattern of unreasonable behaviour.

Desertion

You will need to say in what circumstances your husband left – for example that he simply walked out of the door one day and never returned – and on what date. You will also have to state that he did so without your consent. The fact that your husband is in prison or hospital will not count.

Separation for two years with consent or five years without consent

You will need to state the exact date of your separation.

If you have been separated for more than two years but less than five you will need your husband's actual consent to the divorce. Failing to object is not enough. He will have to sign his agreement to the divorce, which he will do on the Acknowledgement of Service form (see pp 58–59). If you think he is unlikely in the end to go through with it, then you will need either to wait or to find some other fact on which to base the divorce.

If you have attempted to reconcile the marriage then this may affect when and if you can apply for the divorce, as explained on page 45.

Stating what you want the court to do

At the top of page 4 you will see the word 'prayer'. This is the part of the form where you set out what you want the court to do. You will be asked to confirm that you want the marriage to be dissolved – ended – and to state:

- whether you want the respondent, your husband, to contribute to your legal costs (see p 55);
- what kind of financial support (called financial relief) you are seeking (see pp 89–91);
- what kind of arrangements you are seeking for the children (see Chapter 5);
- the names and addresses of the people you want to be served with – sent – the petition. This will be your husband and possibly also the co-respondent.

You will also need to give your home address for correspondence. If you have a solicitor acting on your behalf then they will usually insert their address instead.

If you want to complete the divorce petition yourself without professional help, it is always worth seeking a solicitor's advice about the financial aspects.

The legal costs referred to above are only those directly related to the divorce itself and not those related to other issues such as money and children. For divorces based on two years' or five years' separation it is common for couples to agree to pay half each. If you are petitioning on the basis of unreasonable behaviour or desertion it is usual to ask the respondent to pay your legal costs. In the case of adultery you can ask the respondent and/or the co-respondent to pay the costs. If you are seeking costs against the co-respondent, you ought to discuss this with your solicitor.

Costs are usually dealt with by agreement. For example, a husband might agree not to contest an adultery or unreasonable behaviour petition so long as no order for costs is made against him.

At this stage do not cross off the claim for financial relief. It may be extremely difficult or even impossible to apply for help later on in the procedure if you eliminate it at this stage. If you have agreed with your husband not to make any demands for financial support then you should tell him in advance that you are leaving in the general claim for financial relief and that it will be formally dismissed later on.

Even if you do intend to make a claim for financial relief, you will not need to set down specific amounts at this stage.

As far as children are concerned, although you don't have to say whether you want a residence or contact order (see pp 126–127) on the divorce petition, in practice most people do set out what they want.

Step 3 *Statement of Arrangements for the Children*

This section explains how to complete the special form relating to the care of dependent children. This is a key part of the actual divorce procedure. You should read this in conjunction with the specific information on divorce and children which starts on page 121. Normally only arrangements for children under 16 have to be set out for the court. However, this age limit may be extended if there are special circumstances, for example the child is disabled.

The form (D8A) is eight pages long but it is fairly straightforward and jargon-free. Although the petitioner completes the form it is always best if you and your husband can agree about the arrangements for the future. If you cannot agree between you then you should go ahead and complete the form and let your husband complete a separate one later on (see p 129).

The following explanation of the form is based on the assumption that the children will remain with you, the mother. The form itself is completely even-handed and can be completed by husband or wife regardless of who currently cares for the children.

The form refers to children of the family. This means any child who is:

- the child of both you and your husband;
- any child adopted by you;
- a stepchild who has lived with you both as part of your family;
- any other child who has been treated by both of you as one of the family at any point during the marriage, with the exception of foster children.

In Part II of the form you will be asked to give information about the following:

- where the children live, including the names of anyone else living in the home and their relationship to the children, and whether there will be any change in these arrangements (if you have different arrangements for each child then you will have to state what these are and complete a fresh set of details for each);

- the children's education and training;
- childcare arrangements, including which parent looks after the child from day to day, whether that parent goes out to work, who looks after the children when that parent is not there, who looks after them during the school holidays, and whether there will be any change in these arrangements;
- maintenance – whether your husband pays towards the upkeep of the children and if you have any other source of maintenance. You will also be asked whether the payments are made under a court order;
- arrangements for contact with the children – whether the children see their father and, if so, how often and where, whether the children ever stay over with him, and whether you intend to change these arrangements;
- the children's health.

There is also a section headed 'Details of Care and other Court Proceedings', which asks three questions:

- Are the children in the care of the local authority or under the supervision of a social worker or probation officer?
- Are any of the children on the Child Protection Register?
- Have there been any court proceedings regarding the children? These include adoption, wardship, supervision, access/contact, custody/residence or maintenance.

On the final page you are asked whether you would be willing to discuss the matter with a conciliator (see p 128) if you and your husband cannot agree about the arrangements for the children. You will then need to sign the form. At the very bottom of the form there is a space for your husband to sign his agreement.

Step 4 *Sending off the completed forms*

Once you've completed the forms you will need to send the relevant number of copies together with your marriage certificate (see p 42) to your local divorce county court or the Principal Registry if you live in London. You will also have to enclose the current fee.

You will not have to pay the fee if you are on Income Support or Family Credit. If this applies to you you should also complete an application for exemption from the fees (form D92). Nor will you have to pay if you're getting help under the Green Form Scheme (see pp 48–49).

Step 5 *Serving the petition*

Once the court has copies of your completed petition they will send a copy to your husband – and where appropriate to the co-respondent – using the addresses you have supplied. Your husband will also receive a copy of the Statement of Arrangements for the Children, if there is one.

The court will send out two additional forms. The Notice of Proceedings informs the respondent that divorce proceedings have begun and explains what he needs to do. They will also post an Acknowledgement of Service (form D10). Your husband (and the co-respondent) will need to complete this and return it to the court within eight days of receiving it (see below). If your husband (or the co-respondent) lives outside England and Wales then they will have longer to return the Acknowledgement of Service.

You will receive a Notice of Issue of the Petition (form D9H), which will tell you when the petition was sent to your husband. Form D9H acts as a receipt if you have paid the petition fee. It will also give you a divorce case number – you should always quote this on future correspondence.

The Acknowledgement of Service

This is more than just a tick box to say that the respondent has received a copy of the petition. It also asks about the following:

- whether the respondent intends to defend the case and whether he agrees to a divorce decree being granted;
- where the divorce is being sought on the grounds of adultery, whether he admits the adultery;
- where the divorce is being sought on the grounds of two years' separation with consent, whether he consents and whether he intends to ask the court to consider his financial situation as it will be after the divorce;
- whether he objects to paying the costs of the divorce and on what grounds;
- whether he agrees with the proposals contained in the Statement of Arrangements for the Children.

PAM *'The most difficult part of the divorce process was the letters I got from my husband's solicitor. Even if he didn't want me any more, I couldn't believe he could treat me like this and sanction a solicitor to say such things, like it was my fault I didn't have a job. He appeared to have no appreciation of the difficulties for a woman of my age.'*

Step 6 *Possible problems with serving the petition*

Most of the time serving the divorce petition goes ahead without any hitches. However, problems can arise and the court will usually inform you if they have not received the Acknowledgement of Service.

There are usually two reasons for this: either the respondent has moved away from the address given by the petitioner or he refuses to complete and return the Acknowledgement. You will not be able to proceed with the divorce until he does so, so you will need to take other steps to ensure that your husband acknowledges the petition.

If you are sure that your husband has not moved then the first thing to do is to ask the court for a copy of the Request for Service by Court Bailiff (form D89). This means that instead of the petition being sent through the post, it will be delivered personally by the court bailiff. The form will ask you to send a photograph (if you have one) and a description of your husband. You will need to fill in another form for the co-respondent if that is appropriate. There will be a small fee for each completed form. If you are exempt from court fees and have already filled in form D92 (see p 58) then you will not have to pay. Sometimes bailiff service can result in delaying the process.

If that fails or you don't know where your husband – or the co-respondent – is now living, then you will have to ask the court to waive the requirement to serve the petition. Ask for an Affidavit to Dispense with Service. After completing this you will need to have it sworn before a court official or a solicitor. A solicitor will make a small charge.

If your husband tells you he's got the papers or you've seen them on him or in his house or workplace, but he refuses to cooperate by signing the Acknowledgement of Service, you can apply by affidavit to 'deem' service and so do away with the need for him to return the form.

Step 7 *Application for Directions to Trial and Affidavit in support of Petition*

Providing neither your husband nor the co-respondent, where there is one, intends to defend the divorce, you will be sent a copy of their Acknowledgement along with two new forms for you to complete. (For more information about defended divorce see pp 66–70.) The first form is headed Application for Directions to Trial (Special Procedure) (form D84). The second is called Affidavit in support of Petition (form D80). Both these forms are free.

NOTE You must make sure that you have the correct Affidavit in support of Petition form. There is a different one for each 'fact' or ground on which the divorce can be based.

The Application for Directions to Trial is a very simple form; it is almost like a covering letter for the Affidavit which accompanies it. The form asks the district judge to decide your case. It basically just requires signing and dating.

The Affidavit in support of Petition is longer and more complicated. However, the information you need to provide is presented in a simple question and answer format. Essentially you will need to confirm – and, where appropriate, enlarge upon – the details you have already given in your original petition. It may seem that you are repeating yourself or being asked to go over information you have already given but this is just part of the procedure.

In addition, you will need to provide evidence to show that:

- Your husband – and the co-respondent if appropriate – has received the petition.
- Your husband – and the co-respondent – admits to the adultery, if appropriate.
- Your husband consents to a divorce on the ground of two years' separation, if appropriate.
- Your husband agrees with the arrangements proposed for the children, if any.

In practice a completed Acknowledgement of Service, filled in and signed by your husband, will usually show all of these things. It will need to be attached to your Affidavit, as will the Statement of Arrangements for the Children, if your husband has signed it. These are then referred to as 'exhibits'.

When you have completed your Affidavit you will need to take it along to a solicitor or an officer of a county court who will witness the swearing of it and any other documents. If you can get to the court without too much difficulty you might as well deliver the documents by hand and have them sworn at the same time. Unlike solicitors, court officials won't charge you for this.

What follows is some basic advice on completing the Affidavit in support of Petition, according to which fact your divorce petition is based on.

Adultery

If your husband has admitted adultery on the Acknowledgement of Service then you should identify his signature and attach the document to the Affidavit. Other sworn evidence from third parties giving first-hand evidence of your husband setting up home with another person or going away on holiday with them will usually also be acceptable. In the past solicitors used to instruct inquiry agents to gather evidence by watching the adulterous couple. However, these are seldom used today.

NOTE Hearsay evidence is not usually acceptable. This means evidence based on second-hand or indirect information. For example, a friend could not provide evidence based merely on the fact that your husband had told her about his affair: she would need to have seen the affair being carried on for herself.

Unreasonable behaviour

You will be asked specifically whether the behaviour you outlined in your petition is continuing and, if not, when the last incident occurred. There is also a question about whether your husband's unreasonable behaviour has affected your health; if it has, a medical report from your doctor may be helpful. Alternatively you can simply state how you feel, for example 'depressed'.

Desertion

Once again you will have to say on what date the desertion began. You will also need to state that you did not agree to the desertion and that your husband has not offered to return.

Two or five years' separation

Merely living apart is not necessarily evidence that your marriage has broken down irretrievably. You will be asked to give the date – which may be approximate – when you decided that the marriage was over.

If you have had to continue living under the same roof then you will need to show how you have lived separate lives – for example that you have been sleeping in separate rooms, not having sexual intercourse, eating and shopping separately, and so on.

NOTE The date that you considered the marriage to be over might well have been quite some time before you decided to go ahead with the divorce.

Step 8 *The district judge considers your petition*

The district judge will have to be satisfied that the petition has been properly served on all the people concerned and that there has been an opportunity to defend the divorce. In addition the judge will want to confirm that consent has been given where appropriate. Once he or she is convinced that all the paper work is correct the district judge will do one of three things:

- If the judge believes there is sufficient evidence to support the petition then he or she will give directions for your case to be entered on the Special Procedure list. The judge will then certify that you are entitled to a decree nisi (provisional decree). The court will then fix a date for the judge to pronounce the decree nisi. The business of who pays the costs will also be finalised.

- If the judge is concerned about some of the information given in the Affidavit, then you may be asked to provide a further Affidavit or additional details about certain points. You will be sent a Notice of Refusal of Judge's Certificate (form D79). Usually requests for further information can be dealt with by post but occasionally you might be asked to attend the court in person and discuss the matters raised with the district judge. If this happens your case will be removed from the Special Procedure list and entered on the undefended list.

- If the judge has serious doubts about the evidence you have supplied or the validity of the petition, then again your case may be removed from the Special Procedure list. You will have to make a fresh Application for Directions and ask for a date to be fixed to hear your case in open court before a judge. If this happens you really ought to seek the advice of a solicitor, even if you have been handling your own divorce up to this point.

SABRINA *'I was amazed by the simplicity of the two final court procedures and by the fact that I didn't have to turn up. A couple of letters from my solicitor and it was all over.'*

Arrangements for the children

If you have children then the district judge will also look at the arrangements you propose for them. In particular they will consider making a formal order only if it is in the children's best interests to do so. If your relationship with your husband is amicable as far as the children are concerned, then there is little reason for the court to start making residence and contact orders (see pp 126–127). If the judge is satisfied with the arrangements for your children you will be sent form D84B Notice of Satisfaction with Arrangements for the Children.

However, if there is some obvious dispute between the parents or the judge is unhappy about the proposed arrangements, he or she will usually ask for further evidence. For example, the judge may ask the parents to attend the court for a special appointment or request a welfare officer's report (see pp 128–129). The decree nisi will usually be postponed until the district judge is satisfied that no order needs to be made or alternatively makes a residence or contact order as appropriate.

Step 9 The decree nisi

You and your husband will be told the date on which the decree nisi will be granted. The court will send you a copy of form D84A Certificate of Entitlement to a Decree. This will tell you when the judge will be pronouncing your decree. You won't have to attend the court as they will send you and your husband, together with any co-respondent, a form stating that you have been granted a decree nisi (form 29).

NOTE The decree nisi is only a provisional order and does not dissolve the marriage. You are not free at this point to remarry.

Step 10 The decree absolute

Six weeks and one day after obtaining your decree nisi you can apply to the court for your decree absolute. You will need to ask for a Notice of Application for a Decree Nisi to be Made Absolute (form D36). This is a very simple sign and date form. Unless you are exempt from paying, you will need to include the current fee. Providing everything is in order, you will then be sent your decree absolute (form D37).

If the petitioner does not apply for the decree absolute within three months of being entitled to, then the respondent can do so. However, if you apply for the decree absolute more than 12 months after the decree nisi was pronounced you will need to explain why there has been a delay.

The decree absolute is an important document, so keep it safe. You will need to produce it if you ever decide to remarry.

Future changes in the law

The Government has published a White Paper that proposes to make some fundamental changes to the divorce procedure, for example by introducing 'no fault' divorce. This is to stop couples going ahead with 'quickie' divorces by claiming unreasonable behaviour or adultery instead of waiting for two years with consent. Also proposed is a one-year reflection period between making an initial statement and applying for a divorce order. There is also a great emphasis on family mediation as part of the divorce process. It is planned to introduce legislation in the autumn 1995 Parliamentary session. However, even if it is passed, it will be a number of years before it comes into effect.

WENDY *'Every day when I drove past the court I said "thank you" to myself. I couldn't wait for the divorce to be over. When the final decree came I felt a bit shattered, deflated, flat. Now I was finally on my own. It scared me for a few days.'*

CAROL *'I was bitterly angry when we divorced. I had always found and organised our homes and done all the "good parent" stuff. It seems extraordinary now but I was furious that I had even "found" him my successor.'*

Defended divorce

There are very few instances where it would be sensible to defend a divorce. Defending a divorce can be extremely expensive and all you are likely to succeed in doing is to put off the inevitable. Few defended divorces actually come to court; most are settled outside and a decree is then granted on an undefended basis. It is rare that a marriage can be saved simply by opposing a petition, and the costs and aggravation involved will probably have the opposite effect.

The only point under discussion in a defended divorce is whether or not the marriage has broken down irretrievably. Financial matters and arrangements for the children are dealt with quite separately, irrespective of whether the divorce is defended or not. And don't forget that you can still ask the court to deal with these other matters regardless of whether you actually go through with the divorce.

Remember, though, that long-term financial settlements cannot be enforced until you have your decree absolute.

The fact that one partner feels aggrieved about the consequences of divorce – what happens to the children, the arrangements for your home and other money issues – is not a good reason for defending a divorce.

PAM *'I thought that the person I loved was still "out there". But when he made these awful accusations through his solicitor I decided that the person I had known and loved was "dead". If the person I married still existed the thought of never seeing him again would have been unbearable.'*

Other options

Even if the respondent disagrees with the grounds given by the petitioner this does not mean that the divorce automatically becomes defended. It may still be possible to have the decree granted under the Special Procedure.

The respondent can do something known as 'cross-pray'. This means that whether or not your husband disputes the fact cited in the divorce petition, he can petition for divorce on the same or a different fact. If he does this – while not necessarily denying the grounds of the original petition – and the petitioner does not dispute the cross-petition, then the divorce will be treated as if it were undefended and dealt with under the Special Procedure.

Here are some examples of situations where a divorce might become defended:

- Even if you and your husband have been separated for two years, you may decide to base your divorce petition on your husband's unreasonable behaviour (providing it has continued during your separation – see p 44). Your husband might then deny the allegations and defend the divorce in the hope that you will agree to base the petition on two years' separation with consent instead.

- Your husband might feel that the marriage has not broken down irretrievably and that you have been too hasty in proceeding with the divorce. Denying the breakdown might delay the petition – but not for ever. This could amount to a very expensive 'cry for help' and it may be worth exploring other avenues, for example counselling.

- In adultery cases, where the co-respondent denies the adultery, the divorce automatically becomes defended.

In any defended divorce or where one party seeks to cross-pray, you should always seek professional advice.

Defended divorce step by step

Step 1 Filing an Answer

Your husband will indicate on the Acknowledgement of Service form (see pp 58–59) that he intends to defend the divorce. You will get a copy of the Acknowledgement; keep it somewhere safe – you will need it later on in the procedure.

In addition to the Acknowledgement of Service, your husband will need to complete another form known as the Answer. This is where he will give his reasons for opposing the petition. He can either deny that the marriage has broken down irretrievably or deny the grounds given for the divorce and cross-pray (see p 67).

Your husband should say whether he denies the reasons you have given totally or whether there is some element of truth in them. He may also wish to argue that the alleged conduct was justified.

The form will have to be returned to the court within 29 days and you will be sent a copy. If your husband fails to return the Answer within the allotted time then the petition will remain undefended. He – or the co-respondent – will then need permission from the court to go ahead and defend the case.

If you find yourself on the receiving end of a divorce petition, and you wish to defend it or petition for divorce on other grounds, then you should always seek legal advice.

Step 2 The case goes to the High Court

Once a case is defended it is transferred from the divorce county court to the High Court. The hearing will be in open court before a High Court judge in London or one of the major provincial court centres. In these circumstances you must get proper legal advice.

Before your case is heard in open court, you, your husband and both your legal advisers may be asked to attend a pre-trial review. This will be heard by a district judge. The aim is to see whether you can reach agreement and avoid the unnecessary expense and trauma of a defended divorce.

Preventing or delaying a divorce

(Unlike the other sections the following paragraphs are written from the perspective of a woman respondent, since it tends to be wives rather than husbands who find themselves facing this situation.)

If your husband files for divorce – he is the petitioner – on the grounds of five years' separation without consent, then you – the respondent – are entitled to special protection to ensure that you do not suffer particular hardship as a result of the divorce, for example by losing rights to a valuable pension. This enables you to stop the divorce being granted until full consideration has been given to the financial and other consequences.

Preventing a divorce

In order to prevent a divorce you will need to show that one of two things will happen if a decree is granted:

1 You will suffer grave financial hardship. You will have to show that this would be a result of the divorce itself rather than of the separation or marriage breakdown. Financial hardship in this

context might mean the loss of the right to a valuable widow's pension. This would obviously be of particular concern to anyone divorcing later in life.

2 You will suffer other grave hardship. This is very difficult to define. It might include, for example, becoming an outcast in a community where divorce is not tolerated. However, it is not enough simply to argue that the divorce would cause you immense personal distress or that you consider it to be morally wrong.

In addition you will need to show that it would be wrong in all circumstances to grant a divorce. This means that even if the court accepts that the divorce would create financial or other hardship, it has to be satisfied that taking everything else into account – the interests of the children, the reasons for the divorce and so on – it would still be wrong to grant a divorce decree.

NOTE It is very rare for a divorce to be prevented these days. You may, however, get the decree absolute delayed until the court is satisfied that you have been properly provided for (see below).

Delaying a divorce

Where the petition is made on the ground of five years' separation, you can ask the court to delay granting the divorce until the financial position has been thoroughly reviewed and a satisfactory settlement reached.

NOTE If you want to pursue this you should get professional legal advice. You ought also to be aware that even if the court is not satisfied with the financial arrangements they may still go ahead and grant the final decree if they believe there is a good reason to do so.

Abuse and violence in the home

Domestic violence and abuse is perhaps more widespread than you might imagine. It cuts across all social, educational and religious backgrounds. Behind many marital breakdowns there lies a history of abuse. The abuse may not be the obvious kind, which leaves the woman literally battered and bruised. It may be far subtler: constant humiliation and put-downs, unreasonable sexual demands, the odd violent fight.

The most frightening thing about domestic abuse and violence is that it can endure for years while the abuser and the victim maintain the semblance of a happy family life. The outside world is none the wiser.

There are many reasons why so many women suffer in silence. They may be anxious about their own and their children's safety, worried about where they will go and how they will manage financially, frightened of the consequences of speaking out or concerned that no one will believe them. Above all, after years of abuse and humiliation many women can no longer summon the resistance and the anger to do anything about the situation. If you are told often enough that you are worthless and hopeless, that everything is your fault and you are the cause of every household problem then you start to believe it.

If you are the victim of abuse or violence, you are not alone. It can take tremendous courage to face up to your situation and to tell others about it. But there are sympathetic people you can talk to and the law is there to help you. Although people may urge you to go to the police, remember that it is ultimately up to you to decide what you do.

RUTH *'For years I had not wanted to be with my husband any more. I was desperately alone when I met him after my first husband had deserted me and my young daughter. I was very needy at the time. I didn't pick up on his tendencies to bully and control. In the two years we lived together before we got married he had already given me black eyes and knocked me about as well as shouting in my face very loudly, intimidating me.*

My self-esteem was so low and my need so great that I went along with his swearing he would change and most of the time I tried to forget the abuse that was going on.'

It is very important to ensure that you keep a record of the abuse you suffer. If you are physically hurt in any way, go and see your doctor or visit your local casualty department. Make sure that you are thoroughly examined and that your injuries – and the cause of them – are noted. The same applies to mental abuse if it affects your health, for example if you become depressed or unable to sleep or suffer in some other way. Tell your doctor the truth about why you feel the way you do and make sure it is noted in your medical records.

NOTE You have no automatic right to change the locks on your home and keep your husband out. However, you may be able to get a court order barring him from the house (see pp 75–77), in which case you should be able to change the locks. Always consult your solicitor before you do so.

Going to the police

If you or your children are in immediate physical danger, are threatened or have suffered violent abuse, call or visit your local police station. In the past police officers were often reluctant to interfere in what they regarded as domestic rows. However, attitudes have changed. Many police stations have domestic violence units with specially trained woman officers. At the very least police officers will help take the heat out of a violent dispute and their intervention may provide some respite.

The biggest difficulty for the police is that many women, although they arrive in great distress, are not prepared to give evidence to enable the police to take action. If you are hit or assaulted in any way, then your husband may have committed a criminal offence; for your own protection you should ask the police to charge him.

It may also be reassuring for you to know that your local police are aware of your situation. Sometimes this will ensure that should you need their help later on a 999 call will automatically bring immediate assistance.

The police cannot decide what action you should take. However, they can outline your options and should be able to refer you to a solicitor who specialises in domestic violence and matrimonial work.

Leaving home

By far the best strategy if you are the victim of abuse is to remain in your own home until either an agreement is reached with your husband or the court orders him to leave. However, if you or your children are in physical danger then it might be better for you to leave your home.

Where to escape to is a huge dilemma for many women. What is needed is often a quiet, safe breathing space where you can think effectively and take some action to make your home more secure. A temporary stay with a relative or friend may be the best thing for you, although you may find it hard to ask for their support, especially if they are unaware of the violence. If that option is not open to you then there are other places you can go.

NOTE Whether you own your own home or live in rented accommodation your husband cannot evict you if you leave because of his violence.

Women's refuges

There are women's refuges throughout the country. Their addresses are usually kept secret for obvious reasons. To find out your nearest refuge ask the police, your local Citizens Advice Bureau or library or contact the Women's Aid Federation (address on p 157).

Refuges are usually run by local councils or independent groups of women. Their aim is to offer a temporary safe haven for women and their children who have suffered violence. The refuge will give you advice and information on issues such as where to find a good solicitor, how to claim benefits and how to apply for council housing. They should also offer moral support.

However, refuges vary greatly in the type of accommodation and assistance they can offer. Most are underfunded with only basic facilities. They tend to be busy places with little privacy. For these reasons, if you can, stay with a relative or friend for a couple of days while you seek legal advice.

Council accommodation

Another alternative is to apply to your council as a homeless person. The rules and regulations about who is entitled to help with accommodation and how they get it are complex and bureaucratic. You should get in contact with your council's homeless persons unit or emergency housing office.

The council will want to ensure that you have not made yourself intentionally homeless. You should stress that you have left your home because you feared for your safety. You also need to show that you are in priority need. The council must accept you are a priority if:

- you have children under 16 or under 19 in full-time education;
- you are over 60;
- you are 'vulnerable'. This can include people who are registered disabled, mentally ill people or those with mental disabilities, people approaching retirement and those in poor health.

The accommodation the council provides is unlikely to be very attractive; it will probably be in a hostel or bed and breakfast hotel.

If you are refused help then you can appeal by asking your local housing department for a Section 64 notice. Your local CAB or advice centre will help you to complete it.

NOTE If you are a non-British citizen who came to Britain to marry your husband or you have special conditions attached to your stay, you should get expert advice before you approach the council for help with accommodation. The Joint Council for the Welfare of Immigrants (address on p 156) will be able to help you.

How the courts can help you

There is a special kind of court order called an injunction which is designed either to stop someone carrying out a certain act or to make them do so. As far as domestic violence is concerned there are two types of injunction:

A personal protection or non-molestation order forbids your husband to assault, molest or interfere with you or your children. This includes physical attacks, violent threats and verbal abuse. The order may also require your husband's friends and relatives not to harass or assault you in any way.

An exclusion or ouster order bars your husband from all or part of your home. It may also order him not to come within a certain distance of the house. In addition, he may be ordered to keep away from places you visit regularly, such as your place of work or your parents' home.

Ouster orders can be quite difficult to obtain since they may make your husband homeless. If you have been subjected to a bout of actual violence, you are more likely to succeed with an ouster order if you apply for one immediately rather than when things have settled down.

The penalty for breaking an injunction is ultimately prison.

If your husband has assaulted you and caused you actual physical harm and you think that he might do it again, you can ask the court to attach a power of arrest to the injunction. This means that if he breaks the terms of the order the police can arrest him without a warrant. If you succeed in getting a power of arrest you should take a copy of the court order along to your local police station so that they are aware of the situation.

How to get an injunction

If you have not yet begun divorce proceedings and don't intend to just yet then you can apply for an injunction either in the magistrates court, where the injunctions are known as a personal protection order and an exclusion order, or in the county court where you can apply for a non-molestation or an ouster order.

If you have already begun divorce proceedings or you intend to do so within the next day, you can apply for the injunction to be made in the divorce county court.

Although you can apply direct to the court for an injunction it is best to seek a solicitor's advice. In emergencies injunctions can be obtained after normal working hours and at weekends.

If you don't already have a solicitor ask your local police to give you the name of one who specialises in this sort of emergency work. You can also ask to be put in touch with the duty judge or magistrate.

Injunctions are often made for a fixed period, usually three months. However, if you and your husband are reconciled during this time and begin to live together again then the order will lapse. Unfortunately few violent men actually stop being violent, despite promises to the contrary. Think carefully before allowing your husband back into your home. You may find it more difficult to get an ouster order next time round.

Remember that an injunction is only a piece of paper. Although it may curb your husband's violence, especially if there is the threat of arrest, it cannot actually stop him from abusing you. To make it work, you need to ensure that your husband obeys the letter of the order. If he doesn't you must notify the police or your solicitor immediately.

NOTE Always think very carefully about the consequences of an injunction. If you want to proceed with a divorce, then having a court order barring your husband from the house may not provide a positive start to negotiating the breakup of your marriage. There are other ways to approach the problem, for example by getting your husband to give the court an undertaking (see below) that he will not be violent or that he will leave the house. Your paramount concern must be your and your children's safety, but do talk the matter through with your solicitor.

Getting an emergency injunction

You can get an injunction in a matter of hours without telling your husband. This is known as an ex parte order. If you are successful, your husband will be served with the injunction. However, the court will also fix a date, usually within a week, for your husband to put his side of the case. If he decides to defend himself you may be called to provide additional evidence. The judge or magistrate will have to be satisfied that the injunction is justified.

If they feel it is not, then they may ask your husband to give the court an undertaking not to molest or harass you. Although this means that he avoids having a court order made against him, breaking the terms of the undertaking carries just as severe a penalty as breaking the terms of a court order.

Future changes in the law

There are proposals to streamline the procedure for securing an injunction in domestic violence cases. It is planned to introduce legislation in the autumn 1995 Parliamentary session. The new proposals also extend protection to former cohabitees and spouses who are being threatened by their ex-partners.

4.
Money and the family home

Without a doubt the biggest issue for women separating or divorcing, particularly older women, is money. How will you meet your day-to-day bills? Where will you live? How will you manage in retirement?

Unless you are in a secure, well-paid job and have made adequate retirement provision or you currently have an ample independent pension, you are going to be dependent on your family assets and your husband's earning and saving power to see you through. However, the benefits he has accrued for a comfortable old age may not extend to you once you part (see pp 113–117). Poverty, particularly in older age, is a real issue for many divorcing women. Little consolation as it is, you are not alone.

Talk to any woman who has gone through the experience and you will hear a tale of acute anxiety, sleepless nights and changes in lifestyle and expectations. What also comes through is a fierce pride at being able to survive financially and manage alone. Taking control of your financial destiny may outweigh any drop in income.

Remember, you don't have to wait until your divorce comes through to apply for help with financial matters. In fact you don't even need to begin a petition for divorce. If you have separated from your husband there are a number of ways you can sort out money issues between the two of you, with a solicitor or through the courts.

Even if you carry out the undefended divorce procedure yourself, you ought to take professional advice about the financial aspects of the marriage breakup, particularly as your right to a pension is likely to be a very important issue.

You should start your claim for a financial settlement as early on in the process as possible. If you are petitioning for divorce any claim for maintenance will be backdated to the date of the petition. If your husband is petitioning for divorce and you are the respondent, any claim you make for maintenance will begin at the time of your application.

Even if you agree between yourselves about how to divide up your home and any other assets, you should make an application for financial relief in the usual way. The court will then formally endorse what you have agreed by using the appropriate orders.

Money matters relating to children are dealt with separately in Chapter 5. However, if you are applying for maintenance for your children through the Child Support Agency then this will have an impact on the terms of any overall financial settlement.

NOTE You can get divorced without dealing with your financial situation at all. However, it is very unwise to leave money and property matters unresolved. You ought therefore to consider making financial arrangements as an integral part of the divorce procedure.

CAROL *'Curiously enough, after we split up, although in theory I was worse off, in practice I at last felt mistress of my own destiny. I didn't have to entreat my husband for cheques to pay the bills with. He had paid bills only when we got the final demands and I had lived in constant – and probably foolish – anxiety that we would be cut off.'*

YVONNE *'I found life financially hard once I was separated. By and large I managed to keep out of debt but I had to give up my car. I remember reflecting on how my fortunes had changed when I carried home gallons of paraffin for the heaters in the panniers on my motor bike! Nevertheless*

I did gain some satisfaction from being independent and managing to cope on a very tight budget.'

A note about court orders

The courts have the power to make two categories of financial order·

Financial provision orders deal with money. There are three types of order:

- Maintenance orders: these are orders for payments from one spouse to the other, usually on a weekly or monthly basis. The amount awarded is designed to cover living expenses.

- Secured periodical payments: this means that some assets are put aside and invested in order to produce income to pay one spouse.

- Lump sum payments: one spouse pays the other a substantial once and for all lump sum. This may be paid in instalments.

Property adjustment orders deal with the allocation of the matrimonial home and other capital assets.

You will find more information about these in this chapter.

Thinking about money

You may tell yourself that you find money matters unintelligible, frightening or downright tedious. Or you may relish the cut and thrust of financial dealing and balancing the books. However you feel, if you are going through a separation or divorce you cannot afford to ignore your financial situation.

Before you and your husband – or the courts – can grapple with 'who gets what', you need to have a very clear idea of what assets and income you possess between you and how you each envisage managing in the future. If your husband is cooperative then so much the better, but whatever the situation don't leave it to someone else to establish your current financial position and your future financial needs. Sometime sooner or later it is vital for you to take control – and you don't need to be a banking whizz kid to do so. Common sense will see you through.

A personal financial audit

At some point you will need to draw up a budget. It's worth doing your homework well in advance. Once you've done the real spade work it is much simpler and quicker to revise and bring your plans up to date. Before you get down to drawing up any kind of budget you will need to think about the following.

Your home

- Who owns your existing home? Is it in joint names (see p 107)?
- When did you buy it and how much for?
- Have you made any substantial improvements? If so, what did they cost and who paid for them?
- How much is it worth now? Will it be easy to sell? How much will estate agents' fees be? A reputable local estate agent will give you a rough idea of all these things.
- Is there an outstanding mortgage and what kind is it? How long is left to run and what are the monthly repayments? Ask your mortgage lender if you don't know.
- Is there any ground rent or service charge? If you have a leasehold property how long is there left to run on the lease?
- If you rent your home, in whose name is the tenancy and what kind of tenancy is it? How much rent and other charges do you pay?
- If you have a second home you'll also need to think about its current value and when and how you acquired it.
- Could you manage to run your home on your own? Would it be too big for one person?
- How much could you raise after the sale of the property? (Remember to subtract agents' and legal fees, the outstanding

mortgage, stamp duty and so on.) Would this be enough for each of you to secure a place of your own?

- Could you get a mortgage in your own right? How much would you be able to raise?
- How much would a smaller home cost to buy or rent in your area – or an area you envisage moving to?
- Remember that where you live is not just about balancing the books. If you work or have dependent children or grandchildren or you are disabled, then you'll have other important considerations.

Your car

- Does either of you own a car? Do you own it outright or do you have a loan or is it a company car?
- Who pays for the petrol, insurance, servicing and other running costs? How much do these things cost?
- Do you have any other vehicles such as a motor cycle, boat or caravan? How much are these worth?
- Does either of you particularly rely on the car?
- What would happen if you didn't have a car? Could you afford to run one on your own? Remember you need to be realistic not just about the purchase costs but about the running costs too. An old banger may in fact cost you more per month than something newer and more reliable.

Other assets

- Do you or your husband individually or jointly have any savings or current accounts, stocks, shares, unit trusts, life insurance policies or any other investments? How much are they worth?
- Do you have any valuable paintings, jewellery or antiques? How much are they worth? Were they inherited or given as gifts or bought by one or other or both of you?
- What about your furniture and other household items? It may be worth making an inventory of the major items. This could be

helpful if you and your husband decide to divide them up between you.

Current income

- How much does your husband earn each month including perks? Don't worry if you don't know exactly or if he refuses to tell you. He can be required by the court to do so once divorce proceedings have started.

- How much do you earn? You should have available at least your last three months' wage slips if you're an employee or your recent accounts, tax returns and assessments if you're self-employed.

- Does either of you have any fringe benefits such as private medical insurance or a company car? Do you incur particular expenses associated with your job?

- What State benefits do you receive as a couple?

- Do you or your husband receive a company or personal pension at the moment? How much is it worth each month?

- Do you receive any income from savings accounts, stocks and shares or other investments? How much is it worth?

- Do you have to pay anything for the care of children or older relatives?

- Does either of you make payments to or receive payments from a former spouse or anyone else?

Future income

- Do you or your husband belong to a company or personal pension scheme? Do you know what you will get?

- Could you increase your earning power either by improving your job or by increasing your hours or returning to work? What could you realistically expect to earn?

- Do you intend to take a vocational or other training course? How long will it last and what will it cost?

- If you work will you incur increased costs for the care of children or elderly or other dependants?
- Are you entitled to claim any State benefits?

Debts

Does either of you owe money to anyone other than your mortgage lender? For example, you may have tax arrears, outstanding credit card payments, bank overdrafts or hire purchase agreements. How much is owed?

Outgoings

You should have to hand a list of all your current outgoings – electricity, water, insurance, food and so on. Remember that when you split up and each have your own household, not all your bills will be affected in the same way. Some such as the electricity bill may be reduced; the costs of food and toiletries may be halved (if you live alone); and a few, for example household insurance and TV licence, will remain the same.

Drawing up a budget

To help you draw up a budget, here is a list of items that you should include. Obviously not all the items will be relevant to you at every stage of your life. You will need to be constantly revising your budget. For example, it would be sensible to do one for your current situation and a projected one for after the divorce. You must be realistic about how much it is going to cost you to live from day to day and also to seek some security for your old age. Make sure that all your figures represent either weekly or monthly amounts – do not use a mix of the two or your budget won't make sense.

To draw up a budget you will need to add up your income from all sources and all your outgoings; you will then be able to compare the two. The following pages suggest headings under which you might list your income and outgoings.

Income

Work (full-time/part-time)

Commission/any additional earnings

Maintenance from a previous partner

State benefits (list each one and how much)

Investment income (list each source and how much)

Pension (your husband's/your own)

Other

Expenditure

Income Tax (if not already deducted)

National Insurance (if self-employed)

Maintenance to a former partner or children

Work (travelling/lunch/other)

Your home (mortgage – including mortgage protection plan and other associated costs/rent/ground rent/Council Tax)

Insurance (house/contents/car/life)

Pensions (list each one)

Savings plans (list each one and include regular amounts you put aside for things like holidays)

Health care (prescriptions/dentistry/private medical insurance/permanent health insurance/other)

Outstanding debts (loans/HP agreements/credit card bills/utilities/other)

Household bills (water/gas/electricity/telephone)

TV (rental/licence/cable)

Food

General household goods

Car (tax/petrol/servicing)

School (fees/uniforms/other activities)

Childcare (nanny/childminder/babysitting)

Care of older relatives (residential care/home helps/visiting)

Personal spending (clothes/cosmetics/sport/personal fitness/hobbies/subscriptions/charities)

Entertainment

Holidays (don't duplicate this if it's covered under 'Savings plans')

Transport (other than car)

Legal fees for the divorce (court fees/solicitor/other)

Negotiating your financial position

The more you can agree between yourselves about your financial arrangements, including what happens to any property you own, the quicker and cheaper it will be for you. Your one aim must be to achieve a workable financial settlement. You must be realistic about the resources you have available between you.

Even if you intend to drum out the essentials of your financial position with your husband without professional intervention, it may be well worth seeking some initial advice from a solicitor. This way you will be able to fully appreciate the powers – and constraints – of the court in determining any financial settlement.

Although you don't need to use a solicitor to conduct the actual negotiations – and it will be far less expensive if you don't – you must seek the advice of a lawyer before you finally agree the terms of any settlement. This is particularly true if your husband is inclined to bully you or if he is not very open about the household finances. Where your relationship isn't very amicable you are probably better letting a solicitor (see pp 34–36) negotiate on your behalf.

Alternatively, an independent mediator (see pp 33–34) may help smooth the way to a businesslike discussion between you and your husband.

However, that doesn't mean that you can simply sit back and let others get on with it for you. You will need to supply them with the raw material – how much is currently in the family pot and what you want out of it.

Here are the four golden rules for negotiating a separation or financial settlement, whether you do it yourself or through a third party.

1 Be honest

You both need to be absolutely up front about your financial situation: how much money and assets are in the current relationship, what you intend to do once you have formally separated, and if either of you expects to remarry or set up home with a new partner.

2 Make a sensible proposal

Once you have had a long, hard look at your existing position and future expectations you can make a proposal for a financial settlement. This will include how you divide up your existing assets and whether one spouse will pay the other maintenance (see p 80). If you pitch your proposal too high and appear greedy, you will only succeed in irritating your husband and his representatives. It will probably sour the atmosphere and speed you on to the expense of the courts. On the other hand, you do not want to ask for too little and find that you are unable to manage in the future.

3 Find a compromise

If you and your husband have each considered your respective positions realistically, then there shouldn't be a huge gap between what you propose. If there is, perhaps one or both of you need to think again. Where can you compromise? Could the car or household items such as furniture offset an imbalance in hard cash? If you reach deadlock then you must seek the advice of a solicitor, if you are not already using one.

4 Secure your agreement

If you can agree between yourselves then you can ask your solicitor to draw up a separation agreement (see pp 88–89), or you can use what you have agreed as the basis of a financial application which is part of the divorce procedure. Whatever you do, make sure that you formalise your agreement using the proper legal process.

Finally, one last word. Above all else, don't wrangle over furniture and other household items and family pets. It is a totally pointless exercise which is firmly ruled by the heart and not by the head. Don't do it!

Sabrina *'Apart from worrying about money, the exhilaration of living separately, not being subject to his moods and running my own show gave me a great burst of energy so that I was almost permanently happy.'*

Valerie *'Obviously I was worse off than when I was married. I had to budget very carefully and I had to buy my own car. Emotionally this made me feel good. I was in charge of my own life. If I made mistakes I had only myself to answer to.'*

Getting immediate help

As soon as you separate you can take action to ensure some financial security. You can:

- draw up a separation agreement;
- apply to the court for financial relief.

Which option you decide to pursue will depend largely on the state of your relationship with your husband. If you can agree between you about arrangements then you will avoid the expense and up-heaval of going to court.

Note If you are desperate for money and you are not working or you are working part-time, remember that you may be eligible for State benefits.

Separation agreements

At its most basic, a separation agreement is an informal document written by a husband and wife setting out arrangements for property, maintenance and their children. However, to carry weight it ought to be drawn up by a solicitor and properly signed and witnessed. If you later decide to divorce, you can have the contents of your separation agreement endorsed by the court by means of a consent order (see below).

Although there are no fixed rules about the contents of a separation agreement it is usual to cover the following issues:

- an agreement that you and your husband will live apart;
- what will happen to your home: who will live there, when and how it will be sold, how the profits will be divided;
- arrangements for your children: who they will live with and how often the other parent will see them;
- an amount of spousal maintenance;
- how any assets will be divided up.

Separation agreements are a very useful way of addressing financial matters during a two-year separation. Depending on the wording, they can be challenged in court if your circumstances change. Clauses relating to children can never be binding and can be over-ruled by the court.

Although a separation agreement may look informal you should think about it carefully as the terms of the agreement will lay the foundations for any long-term financial settlement.

If you begin to live together again or one or you remarries or dies then, depending on the terms of the original agreement, the arrangement may come to an end.

Applying to the court for financial relief

Consent orders

Consent orders can be used only if you and your husband agree about money matters. They can be much more comprehensive than court orders made where spouses are in dispute This is because both of you can give undertakings to the court on matters on which the court cannot make an order. Undertakings are enforceable, so you mustn't agree to anything that you may not be able to adhere to in the future.

NOTE For your own protection you should ensure that a solicitor draws up the documents and that you each get independent advice on their contents.

Maintenance

You can apply for maintenance through the magistrates court or the county court. The magistrates court procedure is relatively simple and can be used by women choosing to separate rather than divorce. If you qualify, you may get Legal Aid (see pp 49–50). Once you've started divorce proceedings you can apply for interim maintenance through the divorce county court (see pp 91–92).

THE MAGISTRATES COURT

The magistrates court can make orders for periodical maintenance payments and lump sum payments (see p 80) up to £1,000. You can apply, for example, for a lump sum to cover the living expenses you incurred before the order was made. You can also return to court with further applications for lump sum payments.

You will need to apply to the court by making a complaint, either in writing or orally. You must satisfy the court that your husband has deserted you or behaved in such a way that you can no longer be expected to live with him. In addition, you will have to prove that your husband has failed to provide reasonable maintenance for you. If the court believes that you have a case, they will issue a summons for you and your husband to appear before the court on a certain day.

You will both be asked to provide evidence about your income, expenditure and assets. The court will make a decision based on the factors described on pages 93–95.

If you subsequently get divorced then you will need to include in your petition details of any maintenance you have received through the magistrates court.

NOTE It can take between one and two months to get a hearing at a magistrates court. If you need money urgently you can apply to the court for an interim order to tide you over. An interim maintenance order will usually last for a maximum of three months but it may be extended.

THE COUNTY COURT

You can also make an application for maintenance in the county court. The amount of maintenance awarded in the county court could be higher than in a magistrates court, but the procedure is simpler in the magistrates court.

You will have to submit an application in duplicate together with a supporting statement detailing your financial position and the court fee. Your husband will have to file his response to your application within 14 days of receiving it from the court. A hearing date will then be set and your case will go before the district judge.

Financial help while the divorce goes through

Once you have submitted the divorce petition you can apply to the divorce county court for financial relief. Both petitioner and respondent can ask for financial help at this stage. The court will not be able to make any long-term decisions about lump sum payments and property adjustment orders.

Since the court can only make a temporary order which will last until the decree absolute is granted, the order is known as maintenance pending suit. If the district judge feels that they cannot make an immediate decision about how much maintenance to award, they may make an interim order, which is even more temporary.

You can apply for a temporary maintenance order at any time during the divorce proceedings. The court can backdate any maintenance payments to the time when the petition was first filed.

NOTE If you already have a maintenance order from the magistrates court then you don't need to reapply to the divorce county court unless you need more money than the magistrates court can grant you.

Securing your financial interests

If you and your husband have a joint bank or building society account or any other financial assets in your joint names, you may be concerned about him making off with your savings without your knowledge. To stop this happening contact your bank or building society manager immediately and instruct them to change the withdrawal arrangements so that cheques will be honoured only if they have been signed by both of you. If your spouse is being difficult over access to cash you may want to transfer some money into your own name before you do this.

The court can also help prevent your husband disposing of valuable family assets. Providing you can show that you have a claim to a share in the family assets or income and that your husband is about to make off with them in order to defeat your claim, then the court may issue an injunction to stop him doing so.

If you discover that your husband has already disposed of cash or assets then you may be able to ask the court to have the transaction put aside. If your husband has given them to a third party, such as his mistress, who knew why he was doing it, then you will probably be successful. However, if your husband simply calls up his broker and sells the family shares and then spends the money there is little that can be done.

Long-term settlements

If there are going to be disagreements in a divorce they are likely to be over money and property. However, very few couples actually argue their way into court. The vast majority of cases are settled before they reach the court. Once again, it just isn't worth entering into a protracted quarrel about who gets what. All you will succeed in doing is stirring up animosity and depleting the family resources.

There are no magic formulae by which the court determines how assets are divided. Each case is decided on its own merits. The court will take into consideration all the circumstances of the case. Above all it must take account of the welfare of any dependent children.

The court's considerations

The court will focus on different factors according to the type of order you are asking them to make (see p 80).In general, however, these are the issues that concern them:

- your income and earning capacity and that of your husband now and in the foreseeable future;
- the value of any property and other financial resources belonging to you and your husband now and in the foreseeable future;
- any mortgages or other debts;
- the financial needs, obligations and responsibilities of you, your husband and any dependent children both now and in the foreseeable future;
- your standard of living before the marriage broke up;
- the loss of any pension rights (see pp 113–117);
- your ages and the length of the marriage;

- any physical or mental disabilities or special needs;
- the effect of any order on tax liabilities and welfare benefit entitlements;
- the effect of the Legal Aid Board's statutory charge, if either of you receives help with legal costs, and also the legal costs in each case;
- whether either of you has a new long-term partner;
- the conduct of each spouse.

Most of the above are self-explanatory, but some further information about a number of the points is given below.

Income and earning capacity

The court will consider what each of you is currently earning and whether you could reasonably be expected to increase your income. The court will recognise that if you are approaching retirement and have never worked then you are unlikely to be able to find a job. Equally if you are younger but unskilled you may find it difficult to obtain a secure, full-time, well-paid job.

The court cannot order anyone to take a job. However, if it thinks you or your husband could reasonably be expected to work then they may deem – set – a level of income which they think you could earn and use that as the basis of their calculations. The same will apply if the court believes that either of you is taking a low-paid job or otherwise reducing your income in order to influence a maintenance claim.

The length of the marriage

No one has actually clarified what constitutes a short or long marriage, although short seems to be up to around five years. However, the court will view a marriage of a few years between a young childless couple differently to a relationship of the same length between two people in their 50s.

New relationships

The court will want to know whether you intend to remarry immediately after your divorce – in other words, if there is a new long-term partner on the horizon. This will usually mean that you will be able to share your living and other expenses with another person. At the same time you may be taking on new liabilities and the court will also want to know about these.

Your new partner cannot be required to contribute towards maintaining your former husband. The court may, however, ask for basic details about their income and financial commitments in order to help them assess your claim.

Do not be tempted to lie deliberately or be evasive about your future intentions. If you do, your former husband may seek to have any settlement in your favour overturned.

Conduct

The court will be interested in the conduct of the spouses only if in their opinion it would be inequitable to disregard it. In other words, it may be a factor in their deliberations if, say, your husband's conduct was 'gross and obvious' while your own was by comparison blameless. An affair, for example, will not in itself have any bearing on the case.

A step-by-step guide to making a claim for a financial settlement

Step 1 Completing the application form

If you are the petitioner you will need to complete a Notice of Intention to proceed with Application for Ancillary Relief made in Petition (form M13). If your husband is the petitioner and you are the respondent you should complete a Notice of Application for Ancillary Relief (form M11). Both forms are free from the divorce county court.

On the form you should list the orders you are seeking (see p 80). It is usual to apply for all of the orders so that you leave it open to the court to consider your case fully. You should not, however, state specific amounts of money. These will be decided during the negotiations or, if you cannot come to an agreement, at a court hearing.

If you are applying for a property adjustment order you will need to give information about your home or any other property that you wish to be transferred to you – the address, details of the mortgage, whether the title to the property is registered (see p 108) and so on.

You will need to supply two copies of the Notice of Intention form – make sure you also keep a copy for your own reference. Along with the two forms you will also have to supply an affidavit in support of your application (see below) and the current court fee.

Unlike with the divorce petition, if you are the respondent you do not need to wait until your husband has filed his financial claim before beginning your own.

You may wish to point out to your husband that by making an application to the court you are simply following the run-of-the-mill procedure in divorce. He should not misconstrue it as an attempt to disrupt otherwise amicable negotiations between the two of you.

Step 2 Completing the affidavit in support of your application

The information you give in the affidavit is important because it forms the basis of the evidence which goes before the district judge. You must ensure that:

- The information is complete and accurate – remember that an affidavit is made on oath and false statements constitute perjury.
- You write in the first person: 'I earn . . . '
- You avoid hearsay: you should only state, 'My husband told me' and not rely on 'My friend told me that my husband told her boss . . . '
- You write concisely in short paragraphs and number each paragraph.

The affidavit should contain details about the following:

- your income and savings and your liabilities;
- your intended new spouse where appropriate;
- your monthly outgoings (you should prepare a budget (see pp 84–86) which you may want to use later on in the negotiations);
- your home and any mortgage. Where you have owned several properties during your marriage you might want to include information about each of them – who paid for it, its value at the time it was bought and sold, who contributed to any refurbishment;
- your spouse's income or assets if you think any details might 'slip his mind', for example job perks or valuable personal belongings.

Along with your affidavit you should send evidence to back up the statements you are making, for example your last three months' wage slips or, if you are self-employed, your most recent set of accounts. Each piece of evidence is known as an exhibit. You should refer to each exhibit in your affidavit (and identify it using your initials) and then number the exhibit accordingly. So, say Barbara Brown submits a copy of her last set of accounts, she writes in her affidavit, 'I produce an exhibit marked BB1 being a copy of my business accounts for the last year.' She then labels the accounts 'BB1'. The next item is referred to as 'BB2' and so on.

You can get standard blank forms for affidavits from the divorce county court or a legal stationer. Except in the simplest cases, these should be used as a guide only. If you are using a solicitor, he or she will probably draw up a separate document. Once again you will need to supply two copies of the affidavit and keep one for yourself.

You will have the opportunity later on to respond to the contents of any affidavit your husband files in reply to your application.

Step 3 Filing the application

Once you have completed the application form and the affidavit you will need to take them along to the court. The court office will seal – officially stamp – the forms and hand one back to you. You will need to send this stamped form together with a copy of your affidavit to your husband within four days. Your husband then has 28 days within which to file his own affidavit of means.

NOTE If your husband fails to turn up in court for any subsequent hearing it will be up to you to prove that you sent the documents to him. For this reason you should get a certificate of posting from the post office.

If you are concerned that your husband will not file an affidavit within the time limit you should ask the court for help. They can order your spouse to file an affidavit within a specified period. You can also ask to have the order endorsed with a penal notice. This means that your husband will be in contempt of court if he fails to comply. You must have the order independently served on your husband.

Step 4 Going through your husband's affidavit

Once you have a copy of your husband's affidavit you should go through it carefully. If there are any discrepancies or you want to respond to any of the points raised, you can file a third affidavit. If you think the information he has supplied is false you file another affidavit and so on.

It is quite usual as the case progresses to be asked for further information or evidence such as pay slips, bank statements, a copy of an employment contract, a statement of the value of a pension scheme and so on. This is usually done in the form of a questionnaire; it will be sent via your solicitor if you are using one. If your husband refuses to supply you with this kind of information you can ask the judge to order that he does so.

Step 5 The preliminary or 'directions' hearing

This is an appointment or preliminary hearing with the district judge at which they will give 'directions' about what information they need to have available at a future court hearing. The district judge can ask for specific documents relating to the claims you have made in your affidavit. You may, for example, be asked for a valuation of your home. Some courts issue standard directions when they receive your affidavits. This is the stage at which you can also ask for interim maintenance but the practice will vary from court to court (see pp 91–92).

There is no standard practice for issuing a final hearing date. Some courts will do it automatically, at others you will need to ask. You and your husband will in any case both be notified of the date. If you want to ensure that your husband is physically present at the final hearing in order to be cross-examined, you should ask the district judge for a specific order.

The time you have to wait for a hearing will depend on how busy the court is, but it is likely to be more than three months.

Step 6 Trying to reach an agreement

Once both affidavits have been filed you should consider trying to reach a settlement with your husband. You'll need to send him an offer setting out the terms on which you are prepared to settle. If you have instructed a solicitor this will be done through them.

You can either head your offer 'without prejudice' – this means that the contents cannot be used as evidence in court – or you can head it 'without prejudice save as to costs'; this is also known as a Calderbank letter. If your husband then rejects the offer and the case proceeds to a full hearing, the judge will be told the terms of the offer once they have made their decision. If the original offer turns out to be the same as or more than that awarded by the judge then the person who refused it will often be ordered to contribute to the other spouse's legal costs.

A Calderbank letter can have the effect of bringing matters to a head. If you make a reasonable offer and your husband refuses it, then he runs a very real risk of becoming liable to pay any additional legal costs you incur as a result of having to go to a hearing. However, it works both ways, so try and be pragmatic about accepting a fair proposal to settle. A Calderbank letter can be a bit of a gamble and should be left in the hands of an experienced solicitor.

Remember that if you cannot come to an agreement at this stage and you end up arguing in court, your legal costs will begin to soar.

Step 7 The hearing

A hearing will take place only if you and your husband continue to dispute the financial settlement. Fewer than one in ten financial applications ever reaches a full hearing. Your case will be heard in chambers – in private before the district judge. The hearing will not be open to the public.

You and your husband will each have the opportunity to put your case either personally or through your solicitors. You may also be called upon to give oral evidence, in which case you may be cross-examined. If witnesses are called they will be invited in only to provide evidence; they won't remain in the room throughout the proceedings.

You should prepare carefully for the hearing. You will probably be asked to attend a conference – a meeting with your solicitor and probably a barrister who will represent you in court.

If you are asked to give oral evidence make sure that you listen carefully to the questions put to you. Try and answer them clearly and simply. Avoid becoming emotional or worked up when your husband or his solicitor questions you. The judge will be interested only in the facts of the case.

Step 8 The district judge makes a decision

Once the judge has heard all the evidence and the arguments they may give their judgement there and then. In more complex cases you may have to wait until a later date.

If the judge dismisses your claim for regular maintenance payments then that is final and you cannot revive your claim later. However, you may appeal if you think the decision is wrong (see p 102).

If you cannot be awarded a lump sum immediately because there aren't sufficient resources available but there is a real possibility of capital being raised in the foreseeable future, then the application can be put on one side; you then have the option of applying for a lump sum at a later date. A lump sum application may be adjourned, for example, if it relates to pension provision, since this may well be the largest asset and there is still uncertainty about the status of pensions on divorce.

NOTE You or your adviser should keep a note of the judge's comments in case you decide to appeal.

Step 9 Awarding costs

As soon as a judgement has been made you can ask for costs – money from your husband to cover your legal expenses. The judge will want to know why you think you should be awarded costs, how much has been incurred and whether there was an informal offer to settle (see p 99).

You should go prepared with a rough summary of what costs you have incurred to date. If you are legally represented this will include your solicitor's fees, VAT and disbursements such as estate agents' valuation fees, plus your barrister's fees and VAT. You will also need an estimate of how much representation at the hearing will have cost you.

If you are awarded costs these will usually be on a standard basis. This means that if you have been legally represented you will get only a proportion of your total legal expenses – probably about 60 per cent. Indemnity or total costs will be awarded only in exceptional circumstances, for example if your husband has been particularly vexatious and as a result has caused an unnecessary escalation in the legal costs. Remember, if you receive Legal Aid then recovering costs from your husband will lessen your liability to the Legal Aid Board (see p 48).

Step 10 Registering an order

If you are concerned that your husband may be reluctant to pay up you can register a maintenance order at your local magistrates court. The effect is to ensure that all payments go through the magistrates court; they can then keep a record of whether or not maintenance is being paid. If your husband is not making payments then the court can take action. (For more details see pp 103–104.)

You will need to complete a standard form and pay a small fee for this. The form is then lodged in the divorce county court and sent on to the magistrates court.

Appeals

You can appeal against the decision made by the district judge but you should talk it over with your solicitor. You will need to file a notice of appeal within five working days. If a case proceeds it will go first to the local circuit judge then to the Court of Appeal and finally, though very rarely, to the House of Lords.

Enforcing court orders

Getting a court order in your favour is one thing; ensuring that it is paid on time may be quite another. If your former husband fails to comply there are a number of ways of enforcing a court order.

NOTE If your ex-spouse has disappeared along with your maintenance payments you may be able to get the Department of Social Security to disclose his current address to the court. The court will supply you with the correct form. Try and provide as much information as possible.

Lump sum and property adjustment orders

There are two ways to enforce an unpaid lump sum order. Either you can start bankruptcy proceedings – but these might prove fruitless – or the court can order your ex-spouse to sell assets such as property or shares in order to raise the capital to pay the lump sum. This is usually done at the time the order is first made.

With property adjustment orders the court itself can carry out the relevant conveyancing procedure if your husband fails to comply. In this situation you should seek the advice of your solicitor.

Maintenance orders

There are three ways of enforcing a maintenance order. Unless the order for maintenance was registered in the magistrates court (see p 102), your application for enforcement has to be made in the divorce county court in which the order was made.

A WARRANT OF EXECUTION

The county court can issue an order for a bailiff to seize sufficient of your former husband's goods to raise, when sold, the money needed to pay off the arrears.

To get a warrant issued you will need to swear an affidavit confirming the amount of the arrears. You will also need to complete the relevant court forms and supply a copy of the original order. Fees are charged on a sliding scale based on the amount you are claiming.

NOTE The main drawback is that household goods rarely reach significant sums at auction.

AN ATTACHMENT OF EARNINGS ORDER

This is only of any use if your ex-husband is in regular employment. Your former husband's employer is ordered to deduct a set amount from his weekly or monthly salary and send it to the court, which will then pay you.

To obtain an order you will need to follow a similar procedure to applying for a warrant of execution. You will be asked for the name of your former husband's employers.

Any order the court makes must not reduce your ex-husband's income below what is called the protected earnings rate. This is based on the amount an individual and their dependants would be entitled to if they were receiving Income Support. Allowance is also made for mortgage payments or rent and other essential and long-term payments.

A JUDGEMENT SUMMONS FOR COMMITTAL TO PRISON

If you cannot obtain an attachment of earnings order but you believe your former husband has the financial means to meet his maintenance obligations, you can ask the court to issue a judgement summons.

Although in theory a defaulter can be sent to prison for non-payment, in practice the threat should be sufficient to get him to pay you. If you want to follow this route you must ensure that the application form is completed correctly; it is wise to seek the help of a solicitor.

Change of circumstances: Varying court orders

Circumstances inevitably change, and you or your husband might want to vary the terms of the original order. For example, you or your husband might retire, become disabled or die, or one of you might remarry or cohabit with a new partner.

There are certain types of order that cannot be changed. Neither a lump sum nor a property adjustment order can be varied. However, if a lump sum is being paid in instalments you can vary the size and frequency of the instalments, although not the total amount payable. Nor can you vary an order which was expressed as final and therefore not open to alteration. This will include a separation agreement put in these terms. In addition, if an application for maintenance was dismissed initially, you cannot revive it later.

To vary an order you will need to apply to the court in which the original order was made. If that is now inconvenient you can ask for your case to be transferred. You will need to complete a standard form. You will have to provide an affidavit only if your ex-spouse is slow in responding. There is no fee if the variation is uncontested.

If you have registered a divorce county court order in the magistrates court you will need to go to the magistrates court to have the order varied. Applications are dealt with by the Family Proceedings Panel. Make sure that you have up-to-date information about both your and your former spouse's financial position. The magistrates court is unlikely to have these details and the calculations of the district judge before them.

If you receive maintenance and you remarry then payments from your former husband will cease automatically. If for some reason they continue to be paid, for example because he doesn't know that you have remarried, then he will be entitled to ask you to refund him the maintenance he has paid unnecessarily.

If you are later widowed or separate from a second or subsequent partner, you will not be able to revive any maintenance order paid by your former husband.

If your former husband dies then any maintenance payments he was making will stop. However, if he was paying off a lump sum in instalments, you can apply to his estate for the outstanding amount. You may also apply if he was making secured periodical payments (see p 80), providing the original order did not expressly forbid this. You should make an application as quickly as possible.

EUNICE *'I faced a terrifying cut in income. Through trial and error – mostly error – I managed my financial affairs. After 20 years out of the classroom I could not face teaching so I took various clerical and secretarial jobs, ending up in the Record Office doing archive work which I loved. I'm only just solvent after all these years. It has been a nightmare but only financially.'*

GERALDINE *'My financial circumstances didn't change very much. Funnily enough, although I took on a full mortgage and so on after my husband moved out, I didn't feel worse off even though I was doing* *on one income what had previously taken two. In practical terms I had control over all my money and emotionally this reinforced my feelings of independence. I felt pleased to be managing my affairs.'*

The family home

Most of the information in the early part of this section is for people who own their own home. For the majority of owner occupiers a house or flat not only provides a roof over their family's head, it is also their single biggest asset. If you rent your home, you will find specific information relevant to your position on pages 111–112.

Legal ownership of your home
If you are not the legal owner

Even if you do not legally own the home you have lived in with your husband – in other words your name does not appear on the title deeds – you still have the right to occupy it while the divorce or separation goes through. This means:

- You cannot be evicted without a court order.

- You can return home if you have left for some reason.

- You can have your husband excluded from the property if the court thinks fit, for example if he has been violent towards you.

Once the divorce goes through you may still retain the right to occupy the home. Indeed the court may decide to put the property into your name.

Equally, if you are the sole owner of the matrimonial home, you have no right to bar your husband from living there. In order to do so you will need to go to court (see pp 75–77).

NOTE It is always better to try and remain in the family home if you want to live there permanently in the long run. Some couples, usually because of financial and other constraints, continue to live under the same roof until the decree absolute is granted – and occasionally even afterwards. Even if you lead a completely separate existence, it is rarely satisfactory for both of you to try and remain in the matrimonial home. If you are in this position and things are becoming intolerable, talk to your solicitor before you decide your next move.

If you are joint owners

If you and your spouse own your home jointly it will either be as tenants in common (you each own a specified proportion) or as joint tenants (split equally between you). There is one other important difference between the two types of ownership. If you are tenants in common then when you die your share of the property is divided up according to the terms of your Will or the intestacy rules (see pp 117–118). If you are joint tenants, your share automatically goes to the co-owner, your spouse.

If you are joint tenants you should consider ending this arrangement and sharing your ownership in the property as tenants in common. You can do this at any time by sending a Notice of Severance to your husband. Your solicitor will advise you whether this would be in your best interests.

Protecting your claim to the matrimonial home

If you own your home jointly with your husband then there is no risk of him selling the property without your consent and knowledge – short of forging your signature, which is a criminal offence.

However, if your husband is the sole owner of the matrimonial home you must register your right of occupation. This has the effect of alerting prospective buyers of your interest in the property. Few purchasers would proceed with a sale in these circumstances.

How you register your right of occupation will depend on whether the title to the property is registered or unregistered. If the house is mortgaged your bank or building society will be able to tell you which it is.

In practice the titles to most homes are now registered with the Land Registry. The District Land Registry for your area will tell you how to go about registering your right of occupation.

If your home is unregistered you will need to register a Class F land charge at the Land Charges Department. You can get the appropriate form from a legal stationers. The fee is minimal.

When you complete the forms for a Class F land charge you must write down the name of your husband exactly as it appears on the title deeds to the property. If you don't, the charge will be ineffective. If you don't know how it appears on the title deeds you should cover yourself and write down all combinations of his name, for example, M D Smith, Michael David Smith, Michael D Smith, M David Smith, Michael Smith and so on.

Dividing up the property

Regardless of who actually owns your home or how the ownership of the property is apportioned, ultimately it is up to the court to determine what happens to it when you divorce. Obviously if you can come to some agreement between yourselves without arguing about it in court, so much the better.

If the court is called on to intervene it will usually do one of three things:

1 Order the house to be sold and the proceeds to be divided

Usually this is only practical where the amount of money raised by a sale will provide sufficient resources for each spouse to set up their own home.

When it comes to dividing up the profits of the sale, in a short marriage (less than five years) the court will look at how much each partner put into the purchase and maintenance of the property. In a longer marriage the court is less likely to assess the contribution in purely financial terms. It will consider factors such as whether you have spent your time raising a family and keeping the home going or taken a job to pay other household bills.

2 Transfer the ownership of the property from one spouse to the other

If the court decides that one spouse should become the sole owner of the matrimonial home – regardless of who owned the house originally and in what proportion – then they will usually compensate the other spouse in one of the following ways:

- by allocating them a lump sum – this will really only be possible where there are sufficient additional assets to enable the spouse without the property to acquire their own home;

- by lowering their maintenance obligations or doing away with spousal maintenance altogether;

- by giving them the right to part of the proceeds of the sale of the house when it is eventually sold. The court will specify the proportion they are entitled to.

NOTE If the court does order the transfer of the property from one spouse to the other, it will want to ensure that the person remaining in the home can afford to maintain it. This will be taken into account in the overall settlement.

3 Postpone the sale of the home

This usually happens where the divorcing couple has dependent children, although orders can be made to postpone the sale until the death or remarriage of one of the spouses. The court will set a specified time for the sale. This will usually be when the youngest child has reached a certain age or left home. Once the home has been sold, the proceeds will be divided up according to the terms of the court order.

Transferring the mortgage

Even though the court can order a property to be transferred from one spouse to the other, it has no power to order the transfer of a mortgage. The mortgage lender will have to agree, and unless and until it does so, the person with whom the mortgage was originally agreed will remain liable to pay it.

The lender will be keen to ensure that whoever takes on the mortgage will be able to make the repayments. In some cases, where the wife takes on the mortgage but does not work or does not earn very much, the lender will ask the former husband to guarantee the repayments. In practice the wife is likely to get into arrears only if the husband defaults on the maintenance payments.

You may find that you need to reassess your mortgage arrangements. In addition, if you receive Income Support the DSS may make limited payments towards your mortgage.

If you have an endowment mortgage you should also make sure that you apply to transfer the beneficial interest in the insurance policy. If you don't, you may find that at the end of the life of the mortgage you have nothing with which to pay it off (except by actually selling the property). You will also need to consider what to do about any bonuses that accrue over and above the amount needed to repay the loan.

NOTE In the situation of negative equity – where the value of the home has dropped below the amount of the mortgage – you are faced with a very difficult choice: either you remain in the property, pay the mortgage and hope that the value of the property increases, or you cut your losses and sell the property. If you keep the home, and providing you can meet the mortgage repayments, you will at least retain a roof over your head. Take advice before you make any decision.

Buying out

Another possibility is that you may agree that one of you should buy the other out. In this case the spouse remaining in the home gives the other spouse a lump sum representing the value of their share in the property.

If you intend to buy your husband out, you ought to pay up immediately. If you delay you might find that the value of the property has increased and you need to increase the amount of your payment too. You may be able to finance the buy-out by taking out a mortgage or increasing an existing one.

If your husband is buying you out and there is likely to be a delay in producing the cash, you may be better off agreeing that he should pay a percentage of the equity of the property rather than a fixed amount of money. In the current housing climate, however, you should consider carefully before you decide which route to take.

Rented accommodation

If you live in rented accommodation both you and your husband have the right to remain in your home until the decree absolute is granted. Neither of you can force the other to leave, even if the tenancy is only in one name. The only exception is where one spouse applies to the court to have the other excluded because they are violent (see pp 75–77).

Paying the rent

If your husband walks out on you and the tenancy is in joint names, then both you and your spouse will remain liable for the rent. You should continue to ensure that it is paid regularly. If you are not earning or are on a low income you may be able to get Housing Benefit to help pay for the rent through your local authority.

If the tenancy is in your husband's name only, you can offer to pay your landlord the rent. However, they do not have to accept it from you.

NOTE Whatever the circumstances your landlord cannot simply evict you without a court order. If you do find yourself in court you should explain your situation and ask them to postpone any eviction hearing until the divorce settlement has been decided.

Transferring the tenancy

You can ask the court to transfer the tenancy of the property into your sole name as part of the separation or divorce. However, you must make sure that this happens before the decree absolute is granted. If you don't and the property is in your husband's name only, then you will lose your right to continue to live in your home after the divorce.

Some kinds of tenancy agreement, most notably 'short-term' residential tenancies, contain a clause specifically excluding the transfer of the tenancy. In these cases the court will not be able to act. Always check the terms of your tenancy agreement. If you are in public sector housing you should also find out the prevailing attitudes of your local authority towards these matters.

Pensions

For older women getting separated or divorced, one of the greatest financial concerns is going to be over pensions. There are a number of issues here:

- A great many women approaching retirement age have had very broken careers or may never have been in paid work. Consequently they are unlikely to have made any significant pension contributions in their own right.

- Women in low-paid or part-time jobs may have been excluded from company pension schemes or may not have earned enough to make contributions to either a company or a private scheme.

- Even those women who have contributed to a pension scheme will often have seriously underestimated the amount they need to save in order to provide a worthwhile pension.

- Where a husband has contributed to a company or pension scheme for a long time he is likely to have built up a significant family asset.

- Buying future financial security through a pension or similar scheme can be prohibitively expensive once you reach your 40s.

All of this means that if your husband has accrued a substantial pension entitlement you may stand to lose a great deal of your future financial security by getting divorced.

The courts and pensions

At the time of writing (August 1995) there is little the courts can do to divide up the future gains from any pension scheme. However, they will usually take into consideration any loss you will suffer and try to compensate you. Generally this will be by giving you a larger share of the matrimonial home or ordering your husband to pay you a lump sum so that you can buy an annuity. The real problem arises where the pension is the only family asset and there is nothing else to give you by way of compensation.

From April 1996, however, provisions of the Pensions Act 1995 mean that courts throughout the UK will be *required* to take pension rights into account when making financial provision orders in divorce settlements.

The court will have two options. As before, they will be able to compensate you for your loss of pension rights by redistributing other assets. Alternatively, they will be able to make an order requiring the pension trustees or managers to make payments of part of your husband's pension or lump sum direct to you as 'deferred maintenance' once he starts to draw his pension. If he transfers his pension to a new scheme, perhaps because he has changed job, the order may be able to be transferred to the new scheme or policy.

It is vital to ensure that your husband has made a full disclosure of all his pension assets before any settlement is made. He might, for instance, have AVCs (Additional Voluntary Contributions) or FSAVCs (Free-Standing AVCs) or deferred pensions from previous employers, as well as belonging to his current employer's pension scheme.

These new provisions will apply only to new settlements made on or after 6 April 1996 and then only to payments due on or after 6 April 1997.

Two problems that will remain, despite this change in the law, are that you will be able to receive a pension (or lump-sum payment) only when your husband starts to draw his pension and that the pension will not continue after his death.

Many of those campaigning for improved rights for divorced women believe that the change should have gone further so that the pension could be split at the time of the divorce. This would have avoided some of the remaining problems. The Government has commissioned research on divorce and pensions, and this is expected to be published during 1995.

A new Armed Forces Bill is going through the autumn 1995 session of Parliament which will bring the treatment of armed forces pensions into line with that of occupational and personal pensions.

The treatment of pensions on divorce is a complicated area. The Pensions Act is very new legislation, and we have yet to see how it will be interpreted in practice. In addition, there may well be further changes in the future. So it is always worth seeking specialist legal and financial advice.

The State Retirement Pension

The State Retirement Pension may consist of:

- a Basic Pension paid to everyone who fulfils the National Insurance contribution conditions;

- an Additional Pension, paid under the State Earnings-Related Pension Scheme (SERPS), based on contributions paid since April 1978;

- a small Graduated Pension based on earnings between April 1961 and April 1975.

The amount of pension you are entitled to will depend on your age when you get divorced and whether your pension relies on your own or your former husband's National Insurance contributions or a combination of the two.

Divorce before pension age

If you divorce before you reach State pension age your former husband's National Insurance contribution record can be substituted for your own in order to help you qualify for a Basic Pension or receive a larger one, up to a maximum of the single person's pension (£58.85 in 1995–96). Your former husband's contribution record can replace yours either for the whole of your working life up to the divorce or only for the years when you were married.

You are not entitled to your former husband's Graduated or Additional Pensions.

If you remarry before you reach pension age, you cannot make use of your former husband's contribution record. When you reach 60, if you are not entitled to a full Basic Pension on the basis of your own contributions, you may be able to draw a married woman's pension (£35.25 in 1995–96) on your new husband's contributions once he draws his pension. You may have to wait some years for this if your new spouse is younger than you.

National Insurance contributions

If you are employed and paying National Insurance contributions at the married woman's reduced rate then you will be required to pay at the full rate after your divorce. This is because you will be treated as a single person. You should ask your employer for a certificate of reduced liability or a certificate of election and send it back to your local DSS office.

If you are self-employed and have not been paying contributions because you chose to pay at the married woman's reduced rate when that option was available, you will have to start paying the self-employed flat-rate contributions after your divorce.

If money is very tight and your husband is still working it may therefore be in your best interests not to get divorced unless, and until, one of you wants to remarry.

Divorce near pension age

If your husband is receiving a full State Basic Pension and you are approaching pension age then it may be worth postponing any decree absolute until after your 60th birthday. You may then be entitled to a State Basic Pension immediately on the basis of your husband's contributions. If the divorce comes through before your 60th birthday you may have to pay National Insurance contributions to qualify (see above).

NOTE If you intend to remarry following your divorce you should take advice about the timing of your marriage. If you remarry before you reach pension age you will not be able to claim a pension on the basis of your former husband's National Insurance contributions.

Divorce after pension age

If you divorce once you have reached State pension age and you are not already receiving a Basic Pension you may qualify for one immediately on the basis of your ex-husband's contributions. If you are receiving a reduced pension you may have it increased to the full rate, depending on his contribution record. Your husband does not have to have reached pension age in order for you to use his contribution record. The amount you will get would be the same as if he had died on the date of the decree absolute.

NOTE If you remarry after reaching State pension age any pension based on your former husband's contribution record will continue to be paid. However, if your new spouse's contribution record would give you a higher pension, then you can use that instead.

For further information about all types of pension, see ACE Books' annual publication *The Pensions Handbook* (details on p 161). For information on the State Retirement Pension and other State benefits see ACE Books' annual publication *Your Rights* (details on p 160).

Other financial concerns

Wills

Bequests you made to your husband or instructions that he act as executor in a Will made during your marriage will cease to have any effect once you are divorced.

If your husband dies during the divorce process and he has not made a Will then you are entitled to inherit all or part of his estate under the intestacy rules and vice versa. These are the rules that say what happens to your estate (your property and other assets) where there is no Will. This applies even if you have been granted a decree nisi and are awaiting your decree absolute. Equally, if you have existing Wills and you or your husband dies during the divorce process then the property will pass under the terms of the Will, even if that means that everything goes to the surviving spouse. For this reason, if you haven't made a Will, get one drawn up. And if you have made one, rewrite it.

On the other hand, if you want your former husband to inherit your estate under the terms of your original Will, regardless of the divorce, then you must make this plain, otherwise your wishes will be disregarded after the divorce.

Tax

Separation and divorce may well affect your tax position. These are the main tax issues that you will need to consider.

Income Tax

Income Tax is assessed by the Inland Revenue on your income. This includes money from wages or salary, self-employment, State benefits, savings and investments, and other sources such as income from renting.

Everyone is entitled to a tax allowance; this allows you to receive a certain amount of income without paying any tax. How much you get depends upon your age and personal circumstances. Tax allowances are revised each year in the Budget. There are two key allowances:

PERSONAL ALLOWANCE

Everyone is automatically entitled to this. If you are 65 or over, the amount of the allowance increases, provided your income is not over a certain limit, and it increases again once you reach 75.

ADDITIONAL PERSONAL ALLOWANCE (APA)

If you are divorced or separated and are responsible on your own for bringing up a child under 16 or a child under 18 who is in full-time education, you are entitled to the APA in addition to your Personal Allowance. You must tell your tax office if you are entitled to the APA, otherwise you may end up paying too much tax. If you remarry you are no longer entitled to the APA as you will receive the Married Couple's Allowance instead.

Any maintenance payments that you receive, whether for yourself or for your children, are free of Income Tax.

However, the tax rules for maintenance payments changed in 1988. If you began to receive maintenance payments before 1988, you may be liable to pay tax on at least part of the payment; you should ask your local tax office for their helpful leaflet that explains the old rules.

Capital Gains Tax

Capital Gains Tax (CGT) may be payable whenever you dispose of an asset, whether you sell it or make a gift. Assets might include a house or land (other than your main home), shares, or valuable items such as paintings or antique furniture.

CGT is generally payable on the real increase in the value of the asset over the level of inflation since you began to own it. It is paid at the same rates as Income Tax. Everyone is entitled to a CGT annual allowance. This means that you can make a certain amount of capital gain or profit each year without having to pay CGT.

Some sales or gifts are not liable to CGT, in particular transfers and gifts between husband and wife. However, you must either be living together at the time you make the gift or make it during the tax year in which you separate.

Nor are you liable to CGT on the sale of your main home. So there will generally be no CGT if you decide to sell the matrimonial home and divide up the proceeds.

Problems can arise if one spouse buys the other out of the matrimonial home, or if the matrimonial home is transferred to one of you as part of the financial settlement. The person moving out of the house may find themselves liable to CGT if they move into their new home before the old one is sold or transferred. If you are in this situation, you won't normally have to pay CGT so long as you don't designate another home as your principal residence and the original matrimonial home is sold or transferred within three years.

For further information about your tax position see Age Concern England Factsheet 15 *Income Tax and older people* and ACE Books' annual publication *Your Taxes and Savings* (details on p 160).

RUTH *'It was such a relief to get away from my husband that less money seemed a very small price to pay for this wonderful freedom from fear.'*

DORA *'My main concern was surviving. At first I only sought out people who I knew would approve of me. I didn't mind being single. I had been more lonely in the marriage. If your husband has no money sense it is worse to be broke in a marriage than to have no money when you're on your own.'*

5.
Children

For a divorcing mother one of the greatest concerns will be the welfare of any dependent children. As far as the process of divorce is concerned there are two main issues. The first is who will look after the children and how the other parent, grandparents and so on will maintain contact. The second is about financial provision.

Women separating or divorcing later in life are more likely to have adult or older dependent children. Obviously teenage children will have strong views about the arrangements for their care and will be alert to some of the financial implications. However, it would be naive to suppose that they or adult children will be any less affected by the breakup of the marriage than will much younger sons or daughters.

The care issues

The majority of parents, however acrimonious their own relationship, usually manage to reach a consensus about arrangements for their children. Once again, if you can reach some kind of compromise agreement between yourselves, you will save a great deal of unnecessary aggravation and legal expense, not to mention upheaval for your children.

If you and your husband cannot agree about the arrangements for your children you ought to bear in mind the following:

- The courts will be reluctant to uproot the child and disturb current arrangements if they appear to be working satisfactorily (see p 130).

- Unless there is some serious reason to deny the absent parent contact with the child, that parent will be encouraged to maintain contact.

- Disagreements between parents and a lack of cooperation over care and contact will do little to enhance a sense of stability in the child.

The welfare of your children must be your only consideration. They should never be used as pawns in a divorce or separation. Unless you genuinely believe that your children will suffer neglect or abuse or come to harm in your husband's care, then you need to face the fact that it is in their interests to maintain contact with their father. By the same token, threats that a child will be taken away from their mother's care are usually without foundation, although they instil terror into many women.

Issues relating to money and maintenance often cloud judgements and negotiations about care and contact. It is inevitably difficult to respect a father's wish to have regular contact with his child when he, for example, refuses to meet basic parental obligations such as paying for a school uniform or a pair of badly needed shoes, especially when the mother is facing financial constraints. However, financial responsibilities are assessed quite separately and, where parents are on Income Support or in dispute, quite rigidly by the Child Support Agency (see pp 133–136); there is therefore no real bargaining power in threatening to withhold contact. Contact will not be withheld because of lack of financial support.

GERALDINE *'The announcement that we intended to separate was a tremendous shock to our 19-year-old daughter. She didn't want to know the details. I think she found it very hard to deal with initially. We offered her counselling but she declined. She was at university at the time and we had successfully concealed from her for several months that things were not going well. By the time we decided to divorce two years later she regarded it as a positive decision.'*

MABEL *'My son said, "Not before time mum. You should have divorced him years ago."'*

SABRINA *'We moved from a large five-bedroomed farmhouse to a two-bedroomed terraced house backing on to the railway. They all sailed through their O and A levels and went on to university. My older daughter now reveals that she was much more upset than I thought at the time. She was a challenging and confrontational teenager anyway and she didn't seem to me to change at all. My younger daughter cried when I first told her but carried out the move with characteristic determination and energy. We had fights as she grew up but no more than I would expect. She is quite incredulous about what she remembers of my husband's treatment of me and thinks me incredibly spineless to have put up with it for so long.'*

Talking about divorce

One of the biggest concerns for parents contemplating separation or divorce is the impact on their children, particularly dependent children. For some women it is the overriding concern, perhaps to the detriment of other considerations such as their own welfare. Other mothers look back to the time when their marriage broke up and realise that they were so wrapped up in their own world that they gave little thought to their son or daughter. As with most things relating to children, it is hard to get things right. Every family is different and you may want to take some expert advice if you feel you have particular worries. The following is some general advice:

- Don't attempt to hide the divorce. For many children it will be obvious that something is wrong between you and your husband – even where there haven't been flaming rows. They are more likely to be disturbed by the unexplained – and to jump to all sorts of outlandish conclusions.

- To a greater or lesser extent involve the children in what is happening. You may not want to take them through every step of the process – it may simply not be appropriate – but do seek their agreement to, or at least their understanding, of arrangements that affect them directly.

- Try to give them the opportunity to talk about their fears, hopes and frustrations. It's also important to help them understand how you feel. That doesn't mean that you need to burden them with every last ounce of angst but you should express your own fear or frustration or relief.

- Reinforce a sense of continued love and support for the child. Although you may no longer be husband and wife, you will each continue to be a parent to the child. Many children will blame themselves for the breakup of the marriage or attempt to mend the relationship. It is important to underline that the child is not expected to choose one parent and reject the other.

- Sometimes it's very easy to fall into the trap of watching your child's behaviour and interpreting it all in the light of the separation or divorce. Try to step outside what's happening and ask yourself two questions: 'Isn't that what most other children would do at that age/in that situation?' 'Wouldn't my child have acted much the same had we still been together?'

- If you have the day-to-day care of your child, don't be surprised if you get cast in the 'mean' parent role. It often happens when one parent, usually the mother, does all the mundane cleaning, cooking, taking to school tasks on a limited budget and Dad turns up once a week for the 'treats'. Try to keep a sense of perspective. Most children cannot be 'bought off' in the long run.

- Finally, don't attempt to 'get the children on your side'. It rarely pays and most children are quick-witted and manipulative enough to play the game both ways. Hard as it might seem at the time, it is far better to be as even-handed as possible about the other parent, regardless of what you actually think about them.

RUTH *'Unfortunately I did not realise the great importance of discussing honestly with my children what was going on. I had tried to hide from them all the dreadful upsets, the abuse and reconciliations, the tensions and anger. I thought that if I could just cope with the divorce they would* *not have to know too much or be involved. Of course they picked up on what was going on. I remember being with my son all night as he sobbed, "No divorce, no divorce." This was extremely difficult for me to handle as I felt so much guilt at his upset and blamed myself at the time.'*

YVONNE *'With hindsight I feel that I was so wrapped up in my own unhappiness and misery at that time that I did not give enough attention to my children. This is particularly true of my 15-year-old daughter, who had been difficult for some time. It was only later that I began to realise that her behaviour was probably linked to the tensions between my husband and myself.'*

The Children Act and 'parental responsibility'

The Children Act 1989, which is the major piece of legislation governing children's rights and welfare, including what happens when their parents divorce, introduced some important new concepts. One of the new terms it introduced is 'parental responsibility'. This describes the specific legal relationship between a child and its parents. It sets down the responsibility parents have to care for their child and their right to be involved in its life.

Although parental responsibility lasts until a child is 18, court orders relating to arrangements for children in separation and divorce proceedings will be made for children over 16 only in exceptional circumstances.

Married parents both automatically have parental responsibility. Once an adult has assumed parental responsibility they cannot divest themselves of it (except if the child is adopted and both parties lose any claims on the other). Even if you divorce your husband and the father of your child, neither of you loses your parental responsibility for that child.

Where parents are not married to each other, only the mother automatically has parental responsibility but the father can take steps to acquire it. Other people such as grandparents and step-parents can acquire parental responsibility through court orders such as a residence order.

The courts and children

The decree absolute will not be granted until the court is satisfied with the arrangements for the children. In the vast majority of cases the court will not actually make a formal order, but will leave it instead to the parents to come to an agreement. This means that unless you have to attend for some other reason, for example to sort out a financial application, you won't need to set foot inside the court and the whole process can be carried out through paperwork alone.

The court can make two main types of order:

A residence order This states with whom the child will live.

A contact order This states that the child has a right to contact with another named person.

The court can also make two other types of order:

A specific issue order As its name suggests, this is an order which addresses a particular matter or problem which might arise in connection with parental responsibility, for example which school the child attends.

A prohibited steps order This prevents a person from taking a certain action affecting the child without the court's specific authority, for example taking the child out of the country without the other parent's or the court's consent.

In addition, the court can make certain orders relating to child maintenance (see p 136). Most child maintenance requests are no longer dealt with by the courts but by the Child Support Agency instead (see pp 133–136).

Residence orders and contact orders

Both residence orders and contact orders were introduced in the Children Act 1989 (see p 125). Residence orders replaced custody orders, while contact orders replaced access orders. The aim of the new legislation was to put the emphasis on the child's, rather than the adult's, rights. Orders such as residence and contact orders are made under section 8 of the legislation and are therefore commonly referred to as 'section 8 orders'.

Residence orders are meant to be more flexible than the old notion of custody. Under the new orders it is possible for both parents to have a residence order and for the child to divide its time between the two. However, the court will probably be reluctant to agree to such arrangements if the child's daily routine would be constantly disrupted.

Contact orders stress the child's right to contact with the parent rather than the other way round. A contact order requires the parent with whom the child is living to allow the child to have contact with the person named in the order. That person is not compelled to have contact with the child.

The following people can apply for residence and contact orders: the parent of the child, married or unmarried; the step-parent or former step-parent; the child's guardian; anyone, including grandparents, with whom the child has lived for at least three years (this doesn't have to be the three years immediately preceding the application so long as it is not more than five years before); anyone who applies with the consent of those who already have parental responsibility for the child. Other people may apply in special circumstances.

Residence and contact orders will last only until the child is 16. Any order will lapse if you and your husband are reconciled and live together for more than six months continuously.

Parents who are in agreement

If you and your husband agree about the arrangements for your children then you can proceed quite simply and without any fuss as part of the general undefended divorce procedure by completing the special form D8A Statement of Arrangements for the Children. This is explained in step 3 of the undefended divorce procedure on pages 55–57.

Providing your husband countersigns the form – or at the very least indicates his agreement with the arrangements – then the district judge will probably grant the divorce decrees without further ado.

However, if the judge is not satisfied with the information you have provided or you and your husband appear in fact not to agree, they may seek further information (see step 8 of the undefended divorce procedure on p 64).

Parents who disagree

If it is clear that you cannot agree about arrangements for your children then the court will intervene. There are a number of steps the court can take.

Once you have made an application for a residence or contact order, they can ask you to attend a conciliation appointment. This is usually held in a room within the court with a court-appointed conciliator. You and your husband both attend. Although your legal representatives should accompany you to the court, they may not be allowed into the room during the appointment. If you feel particularly vulnerable, then try to insist that your solicitor comes in with you.

The aim of the meeting is to enable both you and your husband to express your concerns and wishes and hopefully to achieve a settlement. Conciliators should be unbiased and help both parties to articulate what they want to say. If you don't think the conciliator is being helpful then say so.

If the conciliation appointment is not successful, or where it is not available, the district judge will ask you and your husband to submit evidence in support of your individual claims. This will usually consist of the original application, the answer and any witness statements. The judge will also order a welfare report (see below) and you will be given a return date – the date when you will need to come to court so that all the evidence can be considered and a decision reached.

Where parents cannot agree it is usual for the judge to ask the court welfare officer to prepare a special report. Many parents worry that this is something like a social services welfare report and that their fitness to be a parent is under scrutiny. It's not.

The court welfare officer – who is not the same person as the conciliator – usually interviews both parents and also the children. The older the children are the more weight their views will carry. They may also interview other relevant people: the school, a grandparent if they are to look after the child, and so on. The welfare officer will then prepare a report setting out the facts of the case together with their impressions. You and your husband will both receive a copy before you go to court. Again, this is an opportunity for you to try to settle the arrangements before the final hearing. The court may in any case have already set a date for an interim hearing.

There is little to be gained by having a fully fledged court battle over the arrangements for your children. It will simply force you to wash all your dirty linen in public and that will not help either of you. It will be far better to try to sort matters out between yourselves or with the help of a constructive solicitor or through a mediation agency (see pp 33–36).

NOTE If there is a dispute over the future of the children, especially if you want your child to live with you when they are currently living with their father, then you ought to seek professional legal help as early as possible.

The court's considerations

The child's welfare is the court's paramount consideration when it comes to deciding with whom they should live and with whom they should have contact and on what basis. The court has a checklist of issues it must look at when reaching a decision. These include:

THE WISHES AND FEELINGS OF THE CHILD

This reflects the child-centred approach of the Children Act. Older children, who can articulate their wishes, may be invited to come along to the court, where the judge can see them in their chambers. However, if the court suspects that the children have been coached by one or other parent then it is likely to give little weight to the views they express. As far as younger children are concerned, the court's welfare officer will explore their wishes and feelings and reflect them in their report.

THE CHILD'S PHYSICAL, EMOTIONAL AND EDUCATIONAL NEEDS

On the whole very young children or those who have particular needs will remain with their mother. There is an inbuilt bias against removing younger children from their mother's care. However, that is not necessarily true of older children. At the end of the day, it is the parent who has been the primary carer and with whom the child has developed the closest bond who is likely to be granted a residence order.

STABILITY AND THE EFFECT OF CHANGE

The courts recognise that changing an established routine can have a harmful effect on the child, particularly at an already stressful time. The parent who currently looks after the child usually has the stronger claim, therefore. Obviously this doesn't apply where a child has been snatched from their usual home. Courts are also reluctant to split up siblings without good cause.

HARM OR THE RISK OF HARM

A history of alcoholism or violence will definitely prejudice a parent's case, as will a real risk of child abuse. Although a parent's homosexuality will be taken into consideration, it will not necessarily be a decisive factor unless the court believes that the child will be adversely affected.

THE PARENT'S CAPABILITIES

This includes a parent's ability to provide for the day-to-day practicalities as well as their ability to respond to the child's emotional and other needs. The court will be concerned about who can best look after the child during the week and whether weekend visits would be appropriate for the other parent. On the whole the court is interested only in the adult's role as parent and not in their role as partner. They will not be concerned with which parent, if any, was 'responsible' for the breakup unless their behaviour had a direct effect on the child. Having an extramarital affair, for example, does not automatically preclude you from being granted a residence order.

Other issues

Contact with grandparents and other relatives

One of the effects of separation and divorce is that children can lose contact with one set of grandparents or with other relatives or adults who have played a significant part in their lives. Inevitably where there is bad feeling between husband and wife it can spill over into the extended family. This does little to enhance the child's lifestyle. Grandparents and other people (see the list on p 127) can make a section 8 application to the court in the same way as parents. In considering the application, the court will be looking at three things:

- what the applicant is seeking;
- the applicant's relationship with the child;
- the risk of disruption to the child's life.

Contact orders relating to children and their grandparents are likely to be granted. An application for a residence order will probably not succeed unless it has the parents' support or the children already live with the grandparents.

Changing the child's name

You cannot unilaterally change your child's surname even after a divorce. If you have a residence order then you must seek the consent of the other parent or the court if you wish to do so. Even if no residence order exists, the other parent can still object by going to court. The courts tend to be very reluctant to agree to a change of surname. Children who feel strongly about the issue can apply themselves – the court may be swayed by an application from a child.

Holidays abroad

If you have a residence order, you can take your child on holiday abroad for up to a month. If there is no residence order, there's nothing to prevent you doing the same thing. However, if you and your husband are in dispute, you must get his written agreement or apply for a section 8 order.

BARBARA *'I was very anxious that my children should never know how difficult and unpleasant my life had become. When I asked them recently what they remembered of the time my eldest daughter said she felt great sadness that there seemed to be so much misery around. My son recalled he felt really angry about what was going on. My youngest daughter said that she hadn't been surprised.'*

FRANCES *'My sons have always been ruthlessly honest about my shortcomings. They were philosophical about the fact that we were mismatched. The older boy accepts that his father fell in love with someone else but feels disrespect for his long-standing dishonesty and cruelty.'*

HEATHER *'The effect of separation on my 12-year-old son was wonderful, he really bloomed. He relaxed, he could be a kid again and play silly jokes and play-act. He wasn't plucked out of one home and into another. His room at his father's (our marital home) stayed as it was and he made a*

new one with me. We luxuriated – emotionally at least – in feeling
unoppressed. He'd always seen me as the one who managed things
and he took for granted that I'd carry on doing so.'

The financial issues

The Child Support Agency

The introduction of the Child Support Act 1991 has dramatically shaken up the way child maintenance is assessed and collected. The Act and its administrative arm, the Child Support Agency (CSA), have come in for a lot of hostile criticism. As a result the provisions of the Act and the way it is put into force are constantly under review. For this reason this section explains only the principles of the Act and the CSA.

The aim of the Child Support Act and the CSA is to standardise the basis on which child maintenance is calculated and paid. The Act establishes the principle that both parents, whether or not they were ever married, have a duty to contribute to the maintenance of their child. With a few exceptions (see p 136) all financial matters relating to children will be dealt with by the CSA and not by the courts. If you intend to make an application for financial support for your children and you and your husband cannot agree or you receive Income Support, then you must go through the CSA. This chapter assumes that you are the parent with care and your former husband is the absent parent (see below).

NOTE The Act introduced some new terms. The parent or person with whom the child lives on a day-to-day basis is known as the **parent** or **person with care**. The parent who does not live with their child and where the child is being cared for by someone else is referred to as the **absent parent**. Where either one or both parents are absent the child is called a **qualifying child**.

There has been some controversy over the issue of cooperation with the CSA. Essentially if you are claiming a benefit such as Income Support you are required to cooperate with the CSA and give them as much information about your former husband as possible. Failure to do so may mean that you lose some of your benefit. However, you do not have to supply that information if you think that by doing so you will put yourself or your child at risk or cause undue distress.

To find out more about the current provisions of the Act and how they will affect you, you can call the CSA on 0345 133 133, Monday to Friday 8.30 am to 6 pm; calls are charged at local rates. You do not need to reveal your identity if you simply have a general question to ask. They will also send you a form to apply to have child maintenance assessed by the CSA, along with an introductory guide. The form will ask you for extensive information about your family circumstances and income, and also as much information as you can supply about the father of the child and his circumstances.

If you want to find out more about how the Act and the CSA operate, the Child Poverty Action Group (CPAG) produces a reasonably accessible guidebook called the *Child Support Handbook*.

Child support calculations

The rules by which child maintenance is calculated are absolutely rigid and extremely complicated. The amounts set down to meet the everyday 'needs' of parents and children are calculated by the Government according to a strict formula and may not reflect your individual spending. Set out here are the principal stages of the calculation. If you want to attempt to do your own sums you can ask your solicitor or use the CSA literature.

NOTE This formula will not be used to assess absent parents who receive Income Support since they will normally have a set nominal amount automatically deducted from their benefit.

Stage 1 The maintenance requirement

This is an amount of money determined by the Government to cover the daily expenses of the qualifying child. The maintenance requirement does not reflect the actual amount of maintenance that will have to be paid.

Stage 2 Exempt income

The exempt income calculation applies to both parents because they are both liable to maintain the child. Exempt income is the level of income a parent is deemed by the Government to 'need' for their own essential living expenses before child maintenance comes into the calculation. Exempt income includes allowances for, for example, housing costs associated with maintaining a new partner or stepchildren.

Stage 3 Assessable income

This is the amount of a parent's income that will be used to calculate the actual level of maintenance paid. Assessable income is determined by deducting from your net income your exempt income. Net income is your income after tax, National Insurance and half of any eligible contribution to an occupational or private pension scheme has been deducted.

Stage 4 Proposed maintenance

This is the amount of maintenance that the absent parent is expected to pay providing it does not bring his income below the protected income level (see below).

Stage 5 Protected income

The aim is to ensure that the absent parent's disposable income does not fall below a certain level as a result of paying the proposed maintenance.

NOTE If the total amount of your husband's assessable income exceeds that needed to meet the maintenance requirement, he may have to pay an additional amount of maintenance. Once again this is worked out according to a formula and there is an upper limit on the sum that can be paid. If your husband is a very high earner you can turn to the courts for additional maintenance (see below).

Ensuring maintenance is paid

The CSA also offers a collection service. If you think you may have problems extracting child maintenance from your husband you can ask for payments to be made via your husband's employer. In this case the maintenance payments will be deducted from your husband's wages at source.

The CSA will also chase up unpaid or overdue maintenance and may take action through the courts if they think they stand a chance of success.

If you are dissatisfied with the outcome of the CSA's assessment you can challenge it. Do remember, you can only make a challenge if you think your claim has been wrongly assessed and not because you think it 'unfair'.

Additional maintenance through the courts

Although the CSA has taken over the primary responsibility for child maintenance the courts will still deal with certain specific cases. These include maintenance:

- above that which can be awarded under the CSA formula;
- for stepchildren;
- for school fees or vocational or professional training;
- to meet the special needs of a child with a disability;
- from a parent who does not normally live in the UK.

These types of maintenance application should be made in the first place to the Family Proceedings Court in a magistrates court.

GRACE *'My husband thought that our children, aged 17 and 18, were old enough for the separation not to affect them. I knew it was going to affect them as we had had a very strong family feeling before.'*

PAM *'Our children seem to have felt our marriage was over several years before I did. I continually told them what a marvellous father he had been when they were young. I don't think he's said similar things about me. For the first years my son had less contact with his father than my daughter had but this has increased recently as my ex-husband has much more money than me and my son is quite mercenary.'*

6.
Getting through

If only the breaking up of a marriage was like the ending of a holiday – fond memories, perhaps a few regrets and a return to the usual routine. Unfortunately it's not that simple. Having made the decision, or faced up to the fact, that separation and divorce are inevitable, a difficult enough process in itself, you then need to get yourself through the actual business of legally ending your marriage, sorting out your financial affairs and setting up a new life for yourself. And all this might happen at a point when all you wanted in your life was a quiet and predictable future! As we've said before, this can be a time of huge self-doubt; you may question whether it was the right thing to do or how you might have rewritten the past; your legal, financial and social obligations may appear daunting. The experience will be unique to you.

Like many women you will probably discover surprising sources of support and comfort. Equally, those from whom you least expect it may cause you great hurt. You'll get advice from all corners but you are not obliged to take any of it. Greet every achievement with enthusiasm. Treat every setback – and there will be some – as a valuable experience from which to learn and grow and find the strength to meet the next challenge.

JACQUI *'I initially found it difficult to tell anyone about the separation, feeling it to be the mark of personal failure and smarting at the humiliation of rejection. As I gradually did so, I found people's reactions extremely diverse and unpredictable. There were old friends who stepped* *forward and wrote sympathetic letters offering support; friends who had been through a similar experience who seemed glad that the roulette wheel had now stopped at my number; friends whom I had known for years who walked right out of the picture. Perhaps most surprisingly – to me – I found a great deal of support and kindness from people who were basically acquaintances – business contacts, those I met through voluntary work, neighbours, fellow college students.'*

CAROL *'I slowly became my own woman and sorted out my emotional life. After a while I no longer felt it necessary to act in a way that I thought would hurt him if he'd known.'*

In this part of the book you will find some more ideas and tips about how to manage your separation and divorce and make the experience a positive one. You can also read about how other women have coped in the immediate aftermath of a separation or divorce.

Learn to assert yourself

Going through a separation or divorce inevitably means making demands on all kinds of people in all sorts of situations – friends, partners, lawyers, estate agents, utility companies, employers, bureaucrats. If you don't normally think of yourself as someone who makes demands on others, remember that you have a perfect right to:

- ask for information, support and advice;
- state your own needs;
- expect help from lay and professional people alike;
- be treated with respect.

Making an assertive request involves three simple steps:

I **Decide what it is you want or feel** Begin with a clear idea of what you are asking for and what you expect the outcome to be. You should also think about how you will react if the other person turns your request down. Be pragmatic.

2 **Say so, directly and specifically** Try to use phrases such as 'I would like', 'I want', 'Please could you', 'I would appreciate it if you would'. Don't beat around the bush with phrases like 'I hope you don't mind', 'I wouldn't normally ask you', 'I hope you don't think I'm being difficult'. Try also to express your feelings directly: 'I feel much happier when', 'I find this difficult to discuss with you', 'I feel frightened/vulnerable', 'I feel very relaxed'.

3 **Stick to your opinion or request and repeat it if necessary** Don't let others lead you off the point. This is known as the broken record technique and is particularly useful with those who want an argument and faceless bureaucrats who give you 'non answers'. Consider the other person's response but don't let them deflect you into an argument or on to another topic. Steer them back to the matter you want addressed by repeating your original request.

You can also help yourself to appear more authoritative by remembering to:

- look people in the eye when you talk to them;
- walk tall and sit up straight;
- offer a firm handshake;
- not twiddle with your fingers or hop from one foot to another.

Help yourself

There's nothing like a real situation to help you practise making requests assertively. However, to help yourself prepare, imagine what you might say in the following examples:

- asking someone (a man or woman) you meet at a party if they would like to meet you for lunch;
- telling an estate agent that you are dissatisfied that no one has been to view your house and asking what they intend to do about marketing it;
- telling a friend that you found the comments she made to others about your marriage very hurtful and asking her not to talk about it again.

SABRINA *'I found it impossible to tell other people and completely impossible to confide in them. I felt as if I might be confessing to a murder. On each occasion my heart would thump and I would have trouble breathing and speaking steadily. I felt as if I was breaking a dreadful taboo.'*

PAM *'My capacity for aloneness, hard work, separating my public and private life and most of all not talking about it meant I didn't have to keep updating people.'*

Learn to say 'no'

Many women have huge problems with the word 'no'. We have learnt to associate it with selfishness and petty-mindedness, with being blunt and mean and making others feel rejected. Yet much of that is a myth. There is nothing very assertive and self-confident about feeling you have to put others' needs before your own, or letting others dictate what is and isn't important to you. For any woman going through a separation or divorce there are going to be plenty of times when your gut instinct is to say no – times when your family make unreasonable demands on you, when friends want to tell you what to do and think, when people expect you to give more than you want to.

Most of us know when we want to say no even if what actually comes out of our mouths is 'yes'. Our bodies tell us. You probably recognise that sinking feeling in your stomach, the forced smile, the clenched fingers. It really is important to understand that saying no is not unkind or unfeminine. The golden rule to remember is that when you say no you reject the request and not the person. (This may also help you if others refuse you.)

Here are some simple techniques to help you say no.

I **If someone asks you to do something, don't feel pressured to commit yourself immediately** You can buy time. Try saying something like 'I'll need to think it over before I can give you an answer' or 'Do you have any further information? I'd like to find out more before I make a decision' or 'Thanks for asking me – let me come back to you' or 'I need to check my diary first'.

2 **As with making requests, be direct** Say something like 'No thank you, I'd prefer to go alone' or 'I don't want to do that today' or 'I'm not prepared to . . .'

3 **Once you've said no, move on to the next subject** Don't get caught out by following up your direct 'no' by a checking out statement such as 'I hope you're not upset'.

Never feel that you have to justify why you've said no. Other people may feel hurt that you have turned down their request or their ideas but you really don't need to take responsibility for the fact that they sense rejection. It's much better to be honest than to agree to do something and then undertake it in bad grace. You might, however, want to acknowledge the other person's disappointment while sticking to your 'no' very firmly. You could try saying something like: 'I can see you're disappointed but I don't want to . . .' or 'I understand that you feel let down but . . .'

Help yourself

- Practise saying the word 'no' until you feel comfortable with it. Watch yourself in the mirror; try saying it with a smile.

- Think back to the last situation when you said yes when what you really meant was no. Go through it again and practise saying no this time.

- Next time someone asks you to do something or tells you what to think, check your body's reaction. What is it telling you?

Look after yourself

However positive or negative you feel about your separation and divorce, you are going to be experiencing a good deal of stress. Stress in itself is not a bad thing. In fact too little can be just as damaging as too much. What you need to watch for is that you don't become overstressed. Learn to detect the warning signals.

First of all you may notice changes in your behaviour like not being able to sleep or sleeping too much, eating too much or too little, or relying on alcohol or drugs to get you through the day. Secondly, there are changes which affect your outlook such as depression or excessive irritability or a sense of panic in certain situations. Finally, there are physical symptoms, for example headaches, skin problems or stomach upsets. There's no reason why you should experience any of these things. However, most people facing important challenges and new situations will probably identify at least one or two of the symptoms. You can help limit the damaging effects of becoming overstressed by making sure you look after yourself.

HEATHER *'I took a "year out" after the separation – no rushing around, no big projects. I was lazy and let things ride. It did me good. I needed the space to regain my equilibrium. What I did do was dig up my small garden and create a new one. Wonderful therapy – to hell with housework!'*

DORA *'I coped by having a peg board by the front door full of uplifting sayings and lovely pictures to glance at as I went out of the door.'*

Look after your body

Don't become a couch potato. You're never too old to exercise regularly – just check with your doctor first if you're planning anything strenuous. Walk instead of using the car or taking the lift, join a regular swimming or water aerobics class – they're great fun and many are women only. Join a gym or a dance class. Many sports such as rambling or bowls can keep your social life as well as your heart healthy. If you're feeling down, taking exercise will give you a real mental boost. A regular class or visit to the pool or gym will also help give a shape to your week if you're feeling at a loose end and some 'time out' if every hour is crammed with work and family demands.

Visit your doctor for regular preventive examinations for blood pressure, breast and cervical screening and so on. Don't be afraid of seeking a professional opinion if you're anxious about a lump or you feel discomfort. If it turns out to be nothing, so much the better. If there is something wrong, then worrying about it at home won't make it go away.

Finally, make sure that you eat well. If you're on your own and you're feeling low or you're rushed off your feet, it's easy to skip meals and 'make do'. Make a regular date with your family or with friends for dinner or lunch. If you enjoy cooking, you'll have an opportunity to show off your culinary skills. If you want to escape from the kitchen, get everyone to bring a dish or eat out. Sharing a meal is a wonderful way to socialise and cement relationships.

Exercise your mind

Becoming wrapped up in the minutiae of a divorce can dull your senses so keep your mind alert. Join your local library and take a good book to bed. Read the papers and watch a news or documentary programme rather than a soap – it'll give you something to talk about on your next social occasion! Try your hand at a new hobby or craft. Be creative and treat yourself to some new equipment or materials.

Indulge!

The divorce process can be extremely draining both physically and emotionally. Take time to be extra nice to yourself, especially if your ego has taken a bit of a battering. If you've got the resources then take yourself off into the sun, to a health farm or a painting holiday or whatever grabs you. If you would like to find someone to go on holiday with, try contacting Travel Companions (address on p 159).

Whether you fancy dancing the night away on a nightclub floor or an evening in front of the TV with a take-away, do whatever makes you feel good. You don't have to be a millionaire to indulge yourself.

A long soak in an exotic oil-scented bath, a manicure or a trip to the hairdressers can all help put a zing in your step. Put yourself first, make an effort to look good, and you'll help yourself feel good too.

Help yourself

- Set yourself an exercise target and keep a diary. Record what you've done and how you felt, and if you've lost any weight or managed to achieve new exercise goals. Write down the names of the people you meet and any funny incidents.

- When was the last time you visited the doctor? If you can't remember the last time you had a breast examination or a cervical smear test, ask the doctor to check your records and, if necessary, make an appointment. Make sure you go to the dentist regularly.

- Plan a totally wonderful and self-indulgent day for yourself – with or without friends. Book a date within the next two weeks and have a great time!

Manage your time

If you already lead a busy life balancing work and home responsibilities, then the additional business of separating and divorcing will probably have you wishing for at least one extra day in the week. This is particularly true if you now find yourself with all the household decisions to make and tasks to carry out. Too much to do and too little time to do it in is one of the biggest causes of stress. Here are five ways that you can help plan and use your time more effectively:

1 Be realistic about the amount of time you have available. There's little point in agreeing to undertake a million and one tasks if you end up doing most of them rather badly in the small hours. Learn to say no (see pp 141–142).

2 Make a daily 'to do' list. Put down on paper everything you need to do – the big tasks and the small ones. Once you've got them in front

of you in black and white put them in order of priority – the ones that absolutely must be done today and those that can wait until tomorrow (but only tomorrow!). Tackle the most difficult and disliked tasks first.

3 Learn to delegate tasks to other people. Don't ever fall into the trap of thinking that you're the only one who can do the job. You may have to settle for less than perfection – so what if you have to buy a cake rather than make one, the world won't fall apart.

4 Always create some quiet thinking time. Everyone needs a moment during the day to do the really detailed tasks, to plan the next move, or simply to reflect. Make sure that others know when your quiet time is and that they understand that you are not to be disturbed.

5 Cut out the dead wood. Throw out your clothes that don't fit, the UFOs (unidentified frozen objects) in the freezer, the food past its sell-by date, old bills and magazine articles in your desk. File all your letters, forms, statements and other paperwork. Buy yourself a cheap second-hand filing cabinet if necessary. A good clear-out does wonders for marshalling your thoughts!

Help yourself

- Can you find within 30 seconds the following: your last three quarters' telephone, gas and electricity bills; your last six months' bank and building society statements; all the papers relating to your divorce or separation. If the answer is no, search them out. Then commit each one to a special file and store safely.

- Begin by making a 'to do' list right now. Tick each task off as you complete it and keep your week's list to give you a sense of what you have achieved.

SABRINA *'I became quite impressed by my own calmness and ability to make decisions I should have been frightened of like choosing a house and dealing with the builders. I was flying back and forth to the Middle East, holding down a part-time job, taking up a new career in illustration and invading institutions I had never approached before, mixing with scientists and academics without problems, keeping a hand on three* *teenagers and generally coping surprisingly well. I began to realise I could do anything I wanted to. I couldn't believe that I had been so docile and humble for so long.'*

HEATHER *'There was that fleeting moment when I had the keys to my new house and I walked into the bare interior and I thought, "What the hell have I done?" The carpets smelt of dog, the next-door neighbour had reggae music blasting through the walls. I suddenly came face to face with reality. I think I would have burst into tears if my young son hadn't said very matter of factly, "I think we need to start some cleaning, don't you?"'*

SUE *'With the help of my family and friends I have managed to pick myself off the ground and get on with my life. There is still one aspect I have great difficulty coping with – the rejection. Having chosen to remain in my beautiful home town, unfortunately I have to share it with my ex-husband and his much younger new wife. Seeing them together in town even after five years apart I still find very upsetting although deep down I know that my life now is much fuller and more interesting. It hurts that after 40 years someone you have known since your teenage years can't even acknowledge you.'*

7.
Making out

Is there life after divorce? Well of course.

For many women life on their own, with or without a new partner, brings opportunities they never dreamt of in decades of marriage. The challenge of divorce may reveal strengths and desires you never knew you had. Separating in your 50s may mean another 15 years of working life and another 30 or more full of new experiences. Of course it would be churlish not to recognise that some women still have responsibilities to growing children or to elderly dependants and that others are limited by health or financial constraints. Nevertheless, though divorce may be a closing of one chapter it is far from the end of the story.

Few women can afford to sit back and let life post divorce simply wash over them. Getting on with the day-to-day business of living takes energy when you make all the decisions. It's up to you to decide how you live life now.

Work

It's true that the older you get the more difficult it becomes to secure long-term paid employment. If you've never worked and your qualifications are limited, you can be sure that a top-flight, high-paying job is not just round the corner. Don't despair. There are plenty of opportunities for rewarding and interesting employment. What matters is a willingness to tackle new jobs and learn fresh skills. These days it's far more important to be able to turn your hand to a range of tasks. Ask your local colleges about refresher and updating courses or sign up for something completely different. Local employment bureaux may also be able to help you improve secretarial and word processing skills. Don't be afraid of new technology. If you can operate a washing machine, you can manage a computer! If you're interested in going into business on your own, ask about start-up loans and incentives for new enterprises. And don't forget that working as a volunteer with a charity or community scheme not only develops skills and confidence, it may also get you work contacts and possibly a paid job.

JULIA *'The divorce made me more politically and socially aware. I now hold feminist views. Since retirement I have done voluntary work with a Citizens Advice Bureau and I sit on an equal opportunities committee.'*

GRACE *'I was 50 when we separated. I went to the local training centre and they organised a back to work placement for me draughting, which I had been doing before the children came along. I was lucky enough to be employed by the firm after three months. After a few years I wanted a change and got a job as a technician in a local school. I do like the hustle and bustle of the place. I rely a great deal on the company of the workplace.'*

Home and finance

Life on your own probably means your own four walls with no one to argue about the colour of the carpet, crumbs in bed or what to watch on TV! It also means managing your own finances. Despite the popular perception that money is 'men's stuff', most decisions about family finances are made by women. If you have come away from your marriage with any assets, including your home, you must consider how to make the most of what you have and in particular how to provide for your retirement.

Financial planning need not be daunting. You can easily grasp the main trends by reading the personal finance sections of the quality newspapers. If you want to seek financial advice, it is best to go to an independent financial adviser. Many consultants are 'tied', including almost all the high street banks and building societies. This means that they can sell you only financial products designed or promoted by themselves or the company with whom they have links. Independent advisers have a duty to give advice on the best products for you chosen from whatever is available on the market.

ANDREA *'Don't get bitter – life's too short. The best things that have happened to me are decorating my new house as I like it and eating crisps in bed!'*

Love and life

Very few people can survive without the warmth of human company; we all need friends. If you are naturally shy and retiring it can be especially hard to make the effort to make new acquaintances. The important thing to remember is that in every social gathering most people will be feeling as vulnerable as you. The most popular people are inevitably those who pass the time being interested in the person they're speaking to rather than trying to be desperately interesting themselves. A welcoming smile achieves a great deal more than a hackneyed opening line.

However you decide to broaden your circle of acquaintances – through clubs and charities, sports, hobbies, politics or interest groups – friendships take work. After a divorce, rejection can be hard but do remember that for all kinds of reasons some acquaintances will never be more than just that. Quite often the most special relationships – male and female – can happen quite by chance.

Remember, too, that you are never too old to discover or enjoy good sex. Forget whatever pressures are put on you from family and friends: if it feels right for you, it is right for you. If intercourse is uncomfortable – and it's a very common problem – there are excellent new products on the market that can help you, so talk to your GP or your pharmacist. And don't forget that AIDS is no respecter of age. If you or your partner have been at all sexually active then insist that your partner wears a condom. It's the done thing for women to carry a packet with them!

Whatever you decide to do with your life now, believe in yourself. It's up to you to take your courage in both hands and make things happen.

VALERIE *'I had a very casual on-off relationship with the co-respondent but this has ended recently and I do miss him. I don't like to think I have no man in my life and therefore I have taken up an equally casual relationship with someone else. I felt quite comfortable about doing this. I still enjoy sex, I always did.'*

FRANCES *'I always feel the odd one out socially, without a partner. No one to love or plan for, no one to share with . . . Perhaps there never was but I thought there was so I had some security from my fantasy. I anticipate that I will have to make it easy for people to "reach" me socially and learn to give rather than expect.'*

EUNICE *'Divorcing my miserable husband was the best thing I ever did. I now feel my life started from the time of my divorce. It gave me my life back on a plate. I have found myself as they say. When I decided to separate my self-esteem was at an all-time low. I grew stronger and bolder as the divorce progressed and I think I've now become independent, strong and fulfilled. If anything, after the divorce, I think I blossomed socially. I've had several wonderful affairs and unmarried sex was great.'*

SABRINA *'My spirits soared so high with my new independence that I couldn't imagine ever giving it up. Marriage had grown to mean constant criticism and an interfering, domineering companion. The discovery that a husband can be gentle and kind and amusing is a revelation.'*

BARBARA *'Before I become immobile I want to ride by train across Europe, across Russia, across China – and then fly home!'*

Resources

How to use this resource list

Many of the organisations listed here have already been mentioned in the book. Others have been included to provide a source of additional information or support or simply a 'starting point' for further research. Organisations are given under different headings in order to make the list more helpful.

Please remember that organisations do change addresses and telephone numbers. You may need to resort to Directory Enquiries or call another group working in a similar field who may have the new details. In addition, many voluntary groups are under-resourced and their offices may be staffed for limited periods only. Be prepared to leave a message on an answerphone and to call a couple of times before your request is satisfied.

Those organisations with an asterisk* have additional local and regional offices which can be found by looking in your telephone directory.

General advice

National Association of
Citizens Advice Bureaux*
Call the head office to find out your nearest CAB or look in your local telephone directory. CABs can provide information about a wide range of consumer, legal and benefit issues.

115 Pentonville Road
London N1 9LZ
Tel: 0171-833 2181

National Council for
Voluntary Organisations
For details of charitable, voluntary and self-help groups.

Regents Wharf
8 All Saints Street
London N1 9RL
Tel: 0171-713 6161

Mediation and conciliation

National Family Mediation
An umbrella organisation which will put you in touch with services in your area.

9 Tavistock Place
London
WC1H 9SN
Tel: 0171-383 5993

Counselling

Asian Family Counselling
Service
Advice and counselling for Asian couples and families suffering stress in their relationship.

74 The Avenue
London W13 8LB
Tel: 0181-997 5749

Association of Sexual and
Marital Therapists
Send an sae for details of therapists in your area.

PO Box 62
Sheffield S10 3TS

British Association for
Counselling
Can provide a list of counselling services and individual counsellors in your area – send an sae.

1 Regent Place
Rugby
Warwickshire CV21 2PJ
Tel: 01788 578328

Institute of Family Therapy
Offers counselling to families
experiencing psychological, behavioural
and relationship problems.

43 New Cavendish Street
London W1M 7RG
Tel: 0171-935 1651

Jewish Marriage Council
Advice and counselling for Jewish and
mixed-faith couples needing support.

23 Ravenshurst Avenue
London NW4 4EL
Tel: 0181-203 6311
Helpline: 0181-203 6211

London Marriage Guidance
Counselling for individuals and couples
living in London.

76A New Cavendish Street
London W1M 7LB
Tel: 0171-580 1087

Marriage Care (formerly the
Catholic Marriage Advisory Council)
Nationwide counselling service
open to everyone.

Clitheroe House
1 Blythe Mews
Blythe Road
London W14 0NW
Tel: 0171-371 1341

Relate★ (previously the Marriage
Guidance Council)
Local offices around the country
offering counselling to both individuals
and couples.

Herbert Gray College
Little Church Street
Rugby
Warwickshire CV21 3AP
Tel: 01788 73241

Legal organisations and registries

Family Law Bar Association
A similar organisation to the Solicitors'
Family Law Association but for
barristers.

4 Paper Buildings
London EC4Y 7EX
Tel: 0171-583 0497

H M Land Registry
Information about homes on
registered land.

Lincoln's Inn Fields
London WC2A 3PH
Tel: 0171-917 8888

H M Land Registry
Land Charges Department
Information about homes on
unregistered land.

Burrington Way
Plymouth PL5 8LP
Tel: 01752 635600

Legal Aid Board★
Look in your telephone directory for
your local office. They can supply leaflets
about the Legal Aid scheme.

8–16 Great New Street
London EC4A 3BN
Tel: 0171-353 3794

Office of Population Censuses
and Surveys
For a duplicate marriage certificate.
You have to go there in person.

St Catherine's House
10 Kingsway
London WC2B 6JP
Tel: 0171-242 0262

Rights of Women
Provides free legal advice to women.

52–54 Featherstone Street
London EC1Y 8RT
Tel: 0171-251 6577

Solicitors Complaints Bureau
Handles complaints against solicitors.

Victoria Court
8 Dormer Place
Royal Leamington Spa
Warwickshire CV32 5AE
Tel: 01926 820082

Solicitors' Family Law
Association
For details of local solicitors who
specialise in family law. The SFLA has
a code of practice for its members.

PO Box 302
Orpington
Kent BR6 8QX
Tel: 01689 850227

Finance

Child Poverty Action Group
For publications on your rights to
welfare and other State Benefits.

1–5 Bath Street
London EC1V 9PY
Tel: 0171-253 3406

Child Support Agency

Government agency now responsible for assessing child maintenance for parents who receive Income Support and some other benefits and those who cannot agree about financial arrangements.

National Enquiry Line
0345 133 133
24-hour literature line
0345 830 830

National Debtline

Advice for anyone with money problems.

Birmingham Settlement
318 Summer Lane
Birmingham B19 3RL
Tel: 0121-359 8501

Immigration and refugees

Joint Council for the Welfare of Immigrants

An independent organisation which advises on the rights of refugees.

15 Old Street
London EC1V 9RJ
Tel: 0171-251 8706

United Kingdom Immigrants Advisory Service

UKIAS is a government organisation.

190 Great Dover Street
London SE1 4YB
Tel: 0171-357 6917

Gay women

Gay and Lesbian Switchboard

Provides 24-hour national helpline on all topics, including legal, housing, social, health and AIDS.

BM Switchboard
PO Box 7324
London N1 9QS
Tel: 0171-837 7324

Parenting

Gingerbread (Association for One Parent Families)

Self-help organisation for lone parents offering local support groups.

16–17 Clerkenwell Close
London EC1R 0AA
Tel: 0171-336 8183

National Council for
One Parent Families
Advice for lone parents on benefits,
legal matters, practical help and so on.

255 Kentish Town Road
London NW5 2LX
Tel: 0171-267 1361

National Stepfamily Association
Advice and support for anyone who
is a member of a stepfamily including
grandparents.

Chapel House
18 Hatton Place
London EC1V 8RU
Tel: 0171-209 2460
Counselling service:
0171-209 2464

Women in danger

Jewish Women's Aid Organisation
Confidential advice and counselling
for any Jewish woman experiencing
or threatened by physical or mental
violence.

0113 2695885

Rape Crisis Centre★
Support and counselling for any woman
who has been raped or sexually assaulted.

Look in your telephone
directory for the number
of your nearest centre.

Women's Aid Federation
Advice and support, including temporary
refuge, for any woman experiencing or
threatened with physical or mental
violence.

PO Box 391
Bristol BS99 7WS
Tel: 0117 9633494

Companionship

There are numerous social, campaigning and educational groups
offering opportunities to meet new people and expand your
horizons. Here is a selection of organisations which cater to
different types of interests. Why not pick up the phone and find
out more about them?

EXTEND
Keep-fit activities especially for older people. Send an sae for details of classes.

1A North Street
Sheringham
Norfolk NR26 8LJ
Tel: 01263 822479

National Council of Women
Campaigning umbrella organisation open to both national groups and individuals, with branches across the country. Attracts women interested in current issues.

36 Danbury Street
London N1 8JU
Tel: 0171-354 2395

Older Feminists Network
Mostly London-based group for all older women; there is a newsletter published every two months

54 Gordon Road
London N3 1EP
Tel: 0181-346 1900

REACH (Retired Executives Action Clearing House)
For retired professionals who would like to use their skills in expenses-only jobs within voluntary organisations.

Bear Wharf
27 Bankside
London SE1 9DP
Tel: 0171-928 0452

RSVP (Retired Senior Volunteer Programme)
Teams of volunteers nationwide work together on a chosen community project, for example within a local school or hospital.

237 Pentonville Road
London N1 9NJ
Tel: 0171-278 6601

Theatregoers' Club of Great Britain
Operates mainly in the south-east of England through local branches which organise theatre trips to London's West End shows and other places of interest.

55–56 St Martin's Lane
London WC2N 4EA
Tel: 0171-420 3000

Travel Companions

A nationwide service for people aged 30–75 who like to share their holidays. Send an sae for details.

110 High Mount
Station Road
London NW4 3ST
Tel: 0181-202 8478

University of the Third Age (U3A)

Offers courses on a wide range of subjects from academic topics to bridge, rambling and outings to places of local interest. You don't need any qualifications to join. Groups throughout the country.

National Office
1 Stockwell Road
London SW9 9JF
Tel: 0171-737 2541

PUBLICATIONS FROM ◆C◆ BOOKS

A wide range of titles is published by Age Concern England under the ACE Books imprint.

Money matters

Your Rights: A guide to money benefits for older people
Sally West
A highly acclaimed annual guide to the State benefits available to older people. Contains current information on Income Support, Housing Benefit, Council Tax Benefit and Retirement Pensions, among other matters, and includes advice on how to claim them.
For further information please telephone 0181-679 8000.

Your Taxes and Savings: A guide for older people
Jennie Hawthorne and Sally West
This annual publication explains how the tax system affects older people and offers advice on how to avoid paying more than necessary. The savings information covers the wide range of investment opportunities now available and includes ideas for building up an investment portfolio. The book also contains advice on budgeting and managing retirement income.
For further information please telephone 0181-679 8000.

The Pensions Handbook: A mid-career guide to improving retirement income
Sue Ward
Many older people in their later working lives become concerned about the adequacy of their existing pension arrangements. This annually updated title addresses these worries and suggests strategies via which the value of a prospective pension can be enhanced.
For further information please telephone 0181-679 8000.

Earning Money in Retirement
Kenneth Lysons
Many people, for a variety of reasons, wish to continue in some form of paid employment beyond the normal retirement age. This helpful guide explores the practical implications of such a choice and highlights some of the opportunities available.
£5.95   0–86242–103–9

General

Living, Loving and Ageing: Sexual and personal relationships in later life
Wendy Greengross and Sally Greengross
Sexuality is often regarded as the preserve of the younger generation. This book, for older people and those who work with them, tackles the issues in a straightforward fashion, avoiding preconceptions and bias.
£4.95   0–86242–070–9

An Active Retirement
Nancy Tuft
Bursting with information on hobbies, sports, educational opportunities and voluntary work, this practical guide is ideal for retired people seeking new ways to fill their time but uncertain where to start.
£7.95   0–86242–119–5

Life in the Sun: A guide to long-stay holidays and living abroad in retirement
Nancy Tuft
Every year millions of older people consider either taking long-stay holidays or moving abroad on a more permanent basis. This essential guide examines the pitfalls associated with such a move and tackles topics varying from pets to packing.
£6.95   0–86242–085–7

If you would like to order any of these titles, please write to the address below, enclosing a cheque or money order for the appropriate amount made payable to Age Concern England. Credit card orders may be made on 0181-679 8000.

Mail Order Unit
Age Concern England
PO Box 9
London SW16 4EX

INFORMATION FACTSHEETS

Age Concern England produces over 30 factsheets on a variety of subjects, which are revised and updated throughout the year. Single copies are available free on receipt of a 9″ × 6″ sae.

For information about charges for multiple copies and about the annual subscription service, or to order factsheets, write to the Information and Policy Department, Age Concern England, 1268 London Road, London SW16 4ER.

INDEX